PAUL DUNN

Rich Mind, Rich Life

Build Wealth, Overcome Obstacles & Achieving Success

Copyright © 2024 by Paul Dunn

©2024 by Paul Dunn. All rights reserved. No part of this publication may be reproduced, distributed, or transmitted in any form or by any means, including photocopying, recording, or other electronic or mechanical methods, without the prior written permission of the publisher, except in the case of brief quotations embodied in critical reviews and certain other noncommercial uses permitted by copyright law. For permission requests, write to the publisher at the address below.

Paul Dunn Publishing,

Disclaimer: The material contained in this book, "Rich Mind, Rich Life: Build Wealth, Overcome Obstacles & Achieving Success," is provided for informational purposes only and is not intended as financial advice. The author and publisher are not offering it as legal, accounting, or other professional services advice. While best efforts have been made to ensure the accuracy of the information provided in this publication, the author and publisher do not assume, and hereby disclaim, any liability to any party for any loss, damage, or disruption caused by errors or omissions, whether such errors or omissions result from negligence, accident, or any other cause.

This book is designed to provide information regarding the subject matter covered. It is sold with the understanding that the author and publisher are not engaged in rendering financial, legal or other professional services. If expert assistance is required, the services of a competent professional should be sought. Neither the publisher nor the author shall be liable for any economic loss, loss of profit or any other commercial damages resulting from the use of the information contained herein.

First edition

Editing by Marianne Dunn

This book was professionally typeset on Reedsy.
Find out more at reedsy.com

Contents

Welcome – Key Insights	v
Introduction	1
Unlocking Your Money Mindset	5
Notes & Reflections	19
Fearless Finances	20
Notes & Reflections	34
The Habits of Wealth	35
Notes & Reflections	48
Income Acceleration	49
Notes & Reflections	65
Breaking Free From Debt	66
Notes & Reflections	79
Wealth & Relationships	80
Notes & Reflections	93
The Science of Spending	94
Notes & Reflections	108
Mastering the Markets	109
Notes & Reflections	123
Legacy & Wealth Preservation	124
Notes & Reflections	138
Living the Millionaire Lifestyle	139
Notes & Reflections	152
Embracing Your Financial Freedom	153
Notes & Reflections	156

Notes & Reflections 157
Notes & Reflections 158

Welcome - Key Insights

Hi, I'm Paul Dunn, and I'm grateful you took the opportunity to get this book. *Rich Mind, Rich Life: Build Wealth, Overcome Obstacles & Achieving Success* isn't just another self-help book; it's a blueprint for transforming your financial future. As a successful six-figure business owner, I've accumulated valuable experience in running a business, and I'm eager to share how we can all achieve financial success.

You might have tried various methods to secure financial freedom, only to find yourself stuck in a cycle of worry and frustration. Despite working hard, the promise of financial security seems just out of reach.

Perhaps you've read countless books and attended seminars that promise quick fixes to financial woes, but they offer only temporary solutions that don't address the root of the problem. This leaves you more confused and uncertain about your financial future.

Maybe you've even tried changing your spending habits, cutting back on every imaginable expense, hoping to save your way to wealth. Yet, no matter how much you save, true financial freedom remains elusive, making each day a stressful encounter with your bank statements.

Most people aren't taught how to manage or multiply money effectively, leading to widespread financial struggles. The key to financial freedom isn't just making more money; it's about changing your mindset towards money. Shifting from a mindset of scarcity to one of abundance is crucial.

With economic shifts and uncertainties ahead, understanding and adapting your financial mindset is more important than ever. It's not just about surviving; it's about thriving in any economic climate. This book will guide you out of the Financial Frustration Cycle and into a life where money becomes a foundation for freedom.

Introduction

Envision a life where you possess unwavering confidence in your ability to generate wealth—not just financially, but in every aspect of your life. Picture your mindset and bank balance in perfect harmony, driving you toward a reality where you thrive, not just survive. This isn't a distant dream; it's a potent possibility that starts with redefining how you think about money and success.

Cultivating a millionaire mindset is not reserved for the lucky few or those born into wealth. It is a path available to everyone, regardless of current financial situations or socio-economic backgrounds. Embracing this path means shifting your focus from mere survival to creating a legacy of abundance. It's about transforming your approach to life's challenges from reactive to proactive, and from fear-driven to growth-oriented.

True wealth extends beyond monetary gains. It encompasses knowledge, relationships, experiences, and personal fulfillment. Each chapter of your life can be enriched with these forms of wealth if you harness the right mindset. Wealth principles are not just about accumulating assets but mastering a way of thinking that magnetically attracts opportunities and fosters innovation.

The first step is unlocking your money mindset. It's about breaking free from financial fear and the myths society has peddled for years. It's about realizing that money is not an end, but a means to crafting the life you've always wanted. This shift in perception sets the foundation for all other growth. It's not just about making money; it's about making money work for you.

Embracing fearless finances is the next stride. This doesn't mean making reckless decisions but understanding the dynamics of money and learning to navigate its waters with confidence and savvy. It's about building a financial buffer that allows you to take calculated risks—the kind that propels you forward and catalyzes profound life changes.

Developing the habits of wealth is about consistency. Wealth isn't built through sporadic acts of saving or one-off investments. It's crafted through daily habits that compound over time. This means setting systems that automate saving and investing, continuously educating yourself about money management, and staying disciplined even when immediate gratifications beckon.

Income acceleration is not just about working harder, but smarter. It's about leveraging your unique skills and positioning yourself in a way that makes your value unmistakable and your income exponential. This is where innovation meets determination. It's not merely about climbing the career ladder; it's about creating ladders for others to climb with you, thereby multiplying your income streams.

Breaking free from debt is crucial. Debt can be a relentless chain that binds many to a life of limitation. However, with strategic planning and disciplined execution, you can turn your debts into past chapters of your financial story, rather than the ongoing narrative of your life.

Wealth and relationships speak to the fact that your financial journey is not solitary. The people around you can either be catalysts for financial growth or barriers to progress. Cultivating relationships that support and inspire your financial well-being is as important as managing your portfolio.

The science of spending isn't about cutting out all of life's pleasures; it's about spending smartly. It's understanding the value of money in new dimensions—not just in terms of what it can buy, but also in terms of what it can build. It's about making choices that align with your long-term goals rather than momentary desires.

Mastering the markets requires you to not just understand, but anticipate and adapt to the ever-changing world of finance. It's about seeing beyond the numbers and recognizing patterns, trends, and potential disruptions. This mastery isn't acquired overnight but through persistent learning and engagement with the financial world.

Legacy and wealth preservation are about ensuring that your financial success is not a fleeting phenomenon but a lasting legacy. It's about protecting not just your assets but also your values, ensuring they transcend generations. This is where you shift from being successful to being significant.

Living the millionaire lifestyle transcends the cliché images of luxury and opulence often portrayed in the media. It's about living a life filled with purpose, freedom, and joy—attributes that are the true essence of wealth.

As you embark on this journey through the pages ahead, remember that each chapter is not just about reading, but about action. At the end of each chapter, there are pages for notes, providing space to jot down thoughts, reflections, and action steps. It's an invitation to transform your understanding of wealth and success. This book is not just a guide; it's a blueprint for a rich life—a life that you are capable of achieving. Start turning these pages, and start turning your dreams into your reality.

Unlocking Your Money Mindset

"The goal isn't more money. The goal is living life on your terms."
- Chris Brogan

Understanding Your Current Relationship with Money

Embarking on the journey to financial freedom starts with a bit of introspection. It's crucial to understand where you stand financially and what your underlying beliefs about money are. Often, these beliefs are so deeply ingrained that we aren't even aware of their existence. Yet, they dictate our financial behaviours and decisions every single day. Let's dive into your current relationship with money, dissect it, and understand how it's shaping your financial life.

Assessing Personal Financial Beliefs

What do you believe about money? It might seem like a straightforward question, but it's layered with complexities.

Your financial beliefs are the fundamental perceptions you hold about money, influencing how you save, spend, and manage your finances. To start assessing these beliefs, you need to ask yourself a few critical questions:

1. What is your first memory of money?

2. How do you feel when you receive money?

3. What are your thoughts about spending money?

4. What does having a lot of money mean to you?

5. How do you view people who are wealthy?

Your answers to these questions can uncover a lot about your core beliefs. For instance, if you feel anxious when you receive money because you're worried it won't last, you might have underlying beliefs of scarcity. On the other hand, if you see wealthy people as greedy or unethical, you might unconsciously sabotage your financial success to avoid becoming one of them.

Understanding your personal financial beliefs isn't about judging them as right or wrong but recognizing them as the first step towards transforming your relationship with money.

Recognising Limiting Beliefs

Once you've started to identify what your beliefs about money are, the next step is to recognise which of these are limiting your financial potential. Limiting beliefs are those sneaky, often subconscious thoughts that hold you back from achieving your fullest potential. They are the narratives you tell yourself about why you can't achieve financial success.

Some common limiting beliefs include:-

"I'm not good with money."

"You have to work hard to make money."

"Money is the root of all evil."

"I don't deserve to be wealthy."

"Money won't buy happiness, so why bother?"

To tackle these, you must first acknowledge them. Write them down. See them on paper. It makes them less daunting and more manageable. Then, challenge these beliefs. Ask yourself, is it really true? Where did this belief come from? Is it based on your own experiences, or is it something you've inherited from societal or familial expectations?

By questioning your limiting beliefs, you start to loosen their grip on your financial decisions. This process isn't overnight magic; it's a thoughtful exploration that requires patience and persistence.

Impact of Upbringing on Money Attitudes

Your upbringing plays a pivotal role in shaping your attitudes towards money. The environment you grew up in, the financial habits of your family, and the economic conditions during your formative years all contribute to your current financial paradigm.

If money was a constant source of conflict in your family, you might have grown up with anxiety surrounding financial discussions. If your family lived paycheck to paycheck, you might have ingrained a scarcity mindset, perpetually worried that there will never be enough. Conversely, if you were raised in a financially abundant household, you might either see wealth as a normal part of life or feel pressure to live up to the financial success of your predecessors.

Reflecting on your upbringing and its impact on your money attitudes is not about placing blame but understanding context. It's about recognising that while your financial education began at home, it doesn't have to end there. You have the power to reshape your financial future based on new beliefs and knowledge.

This exploration into your current relationship with money is the first step towards cultivating a millionaire mindset. By assessing your personal financial beliefs, recognising limiting beliefs, and understanding the impact of your upbringing, you are setting the stage for profound changes in how you interact with money. This isn't just about increasing your bank balance; it's about transforming your life by redefining your financial identity. As you continue to delve deeper into these areas, keep an open mind and be ready to challenge what you thought you knew about money. Your path to financial freedom is not just about learning new strategies but unlearning old ones that no longer serve you.

The Psychology of Wealth

When diving into the concept of wealth, it's crucial to start with the mind. How you perceive wealth fundamentally shapes your ability to acquire and sustain it. Let's unravel some of these mental threads and see how they tie into your financial fabric.

Abundance vs Scarcity Mindset

Picture two people: one views the world as a treasure chest, overflowing with opportunities. The other sees it as a finite pie, where every slice taken by someone means less for everyone else. These perspectives are classic examples of the 'abundance mindset' and the 'scarcity mindset'.

If you operate from an abundance mindset, you believe there are always more opportunities and resources available. This belief fuels a sense of possibility and encourages risk-taking and investment, which are essential for wealth creation. You tend to collaborate more, share ideas, and believe that mutual success is achievable. This openness not only attracts opportunities but also fosters a network of relationships that can propel you forward financially.

On the flip side, a scarcity mindset can significantly hold you back. If you view resources as limited, fear and anxiety creep in, leading to overly conservative financial decisions. You might hoard resources or avoid investments due to fear of loss, missing out on lucrative opportunities. This mindset can lead to a zero-sum game mentality, where you believe that for you to win, someone else must lose, restricting the flow of wealth into your life.

To cultivate an abundance mindset, start by acknowledging and celebrating others' successes. Understand that their achievements don't limit your potential. Engage in activities that expand your sense of possibility, like networking or mentoring. Reflect on times when you have successfully seized opportunities, reinforcing the belief that more are on the way.

Cognitive Biases Affecting Wealth

Our brains are wired with shortcuts known as cognitive biases. These biases can skew reasoning and affect your financial decisions, often without you even realising it.

One common bias is the 'confirmation bias', where you favour information that confirms your existing beliefs. If you believe that investing is inherently risky, you're more likely to notice information that supports this belief, ignoring evidence of safe investment strategies. This can prevent you from building your wealth through informed, diverse investments.

Another bias is 'loss aversion', a tendency to prefer avoiding losses rather than acquiring equivalent gains. For example, the pain of losing £100 is psychologically more impactful than the pleasure of gaining £100. This can make you overly cautious, avoiding potentially profitable investments just because they carry risk.

To counteract these biases, strive towards becoming more self-aware. Question your decisions and beliefs by asking, "Why do I think this way?" Seek out information from multiple sources to challenge your preconceptions. This broader, more balanced view can lead to smarter financial decisions.

Psychological Barriers to Earning More

Several psychological barriers can prevent you from increasing your earnings. These include fear of failure, imposter syndrome, and a fixed mindset.

Fear of failure is particularly paralysing. It can prevent you from taking necessary risks or trying new ventures. Remember, every successful entrepreneur has failed at some point. Instead of viewing failure as a setback, see it as a stepping stone towards greater success. Embrace failures as lessons that sharpen your decision-making skills.

Imposter syndrome can also be a significant barrier. This is where you believe you're not truly deserving of success or that you're a 'fraud' despite evident successes. This can prevent you from seeking higher-paying roles or negotiating your salary. To combat this, keep a record of your accomplishments and the positive feedback you've received. This evidence can bolster your confidence and help you internalise your successes.

Lastly, a fixed mindset – the belief that your abilities are static and unchangeable – can hinder your financial growth. Embrace a growth mindset instead, the belief that you can develop and enhance your abilities through dedication and hard work. This mindset encourages learning and resilience, both critical for financial success.

By understanding these psychological aspects of wealth, you can start to dismantle the barriers that have held you back. Remember, the journey to financial freedom begins in the mind. By shifting your mindset, challenging your biases, and overcoming psychological barriers, you pave the way toward not just achieving wealth, but sustaining and growing it as well.

Setting the Foundation for Change

Importance of Financial Literacy

Let's kick things off with a fundamental truth: you can't manage what you don't understand. Financial literacy is more than just a buzzword; it's an essential toolset that empowers you to make informed decisions about your money. Think of it as learning a new language—the language of money. Once you're fluent, you're better equipped to navigate the financial world, from interpreting interest rates to understanding the fine print of a mortgage and spotting investment opportunities that align with your financial goals.

Why is financial literacy crucial, you ask? Well, it boils down to control. With financial knowledge, you take control of your finances rather than letting them control you. You can dodge common pitfalls like over-borrowing, falling into debt traps, or missing out on benefits of investments that could multiply your wealth. Moreover, understanding financial principles helps you set realistic expectations and measure your progress accurately.

Start building your financial literacy by focusing on key concepts such as budgeting, investing, managing debts, and understanding taxes and insurance. There are plenty of resources out there—books, podcasts, blogs, and even free online courses. Make it a goal to learn something new about finances every week. The more you know, the better your decisions will be.

Creating a Personal Finance Vision

Now, imagine your ideal financial scenario. What does it look like? Are you debt-free, funding your dream business, or preparing for early retirement? This vision is crucial because it acts as a guiding star for your financial decisions. Without it, you risk wandering aimlessly or, worse, making choices that contradict your long-term objectives.

Creating a personal finance vision involves setting clear, achievable goals. Start with broad aspirations and then break them down into specific, measurable, achievable, relevant, and time-bound (SMART) goals. For instance, instead of vaguely aiming to 'save more money', set a goal to 'save £500 a month for the next year towards a deposit on a house'.

Your financial vision should also reflect your values—what truly matters to you. Is financial security more important, or are you willing to take risks for potentially higher returns? Do you value experiences over possessions? Aligning your financial goals with your personal values brings not only clarity but also a sense of satisfaction and purpose in how you manage your finances.

Visualisation can be a powerful tool here. Regularly visualising achieving your financial goals can boost your motivation and commitment. Whether it's a vision board or a detailed spreadsheet, choose a method that resonates with you and keep your financial vision visible and central in your daily life.

Initial Steps Towards a Positive Money Mindset

Finally, let's talk about shifting your mindset. Your mindset shapes your financial reality. It's not just about thinking positively but about cultivating a mindset that views challenges as opportunities and setbacks as lessons. The transition to a positive money mindset begins with awareness and is sustained by practice and persistence.

Start by observing your thoughts and feelings about money. Do you feel anxious when checking your bank statements? Do you get excited or fearful when thinking about investing? These reactions are clues to your underlying beliefs about money. Challenge any negative or limiting beliefs by asking yourself, "Is this really true?" or "Is there evidence to support this belief, or is it an old narrative that no longer serves me?"

Next, practice gratitude. It might sound cliché, but acknowledging what you already have can significantly shift your focus from scarcity to abundance. Make it a habit to list down at least three financial blessings every day, whether it's having a job, owning a home, or simply being able to pay your bills. This habit not only fosters positivity but also attracts more abundance into your life.

Lastly, commit to lifelong learning. The world of finance is always evolving, and keeping up-to-date with new information and trends will help you make better decisions. Engage with financial communities online, attend workshops, or consult with financial advisors. Every step you take towards increasing your knowledge reinforces a positive money mindset.

By focusing on these foundational aspects of financial literacy, crafting a personal finance vision, and cultivating a positive money mindset, you're setting the stage for not just financial freedom but a richer, more fulfilling life. Remember, every small step you take is a piece of the puzzle in achieving your financial dreams. Embrace the journey, and let each day bring you closer to the life you envision.

Summary and Application Exercises

Congratulations on taking this deep dive into your money mindset! By now, you've embarked on a crucial journey to understand your current relationship with money, explored the psychological underpinnings of wealth, and have set foundational stones for change. Let's solidify what you've learnt with actionable steps to transform these insights into tangible outcomes.

First, reflect on your personal financial beliefs and recognise any limiting beliefs that may be holding you back. Write these down and openly challenge each one. Ask yourself, "Is this belief based on facts or assumptions?" and "How has this belief shaped my financial decisions?" This exercise is not just enlightening; it's a stepping stone to rewriting your financial story.

Next, shift your focus from a scarcity to an abundance mindset.

Begin each day by noting down at least one opportunity for growth or gratitude related to your finances. This could be as simple as appreciating a steady income or recognising a new investment opportunity. This daily practice pivots your brain from focusing on lack to recognising abundance, gradually rewiring your thought patterns towards wealth accumulation.

Address cognitive biases and psychological barriers by educating yourself further. Pick up books on behavioural finance, or subscribe to podcasts that tackle these themes. Understanding the 'why' behind your financial decisions makes it easier to navigate and rectify them.

Now, let's talk about setting the groundwork for lasting change. Ensure you're financially literate; understand basic financial principles and how the market operates. Utilise resources like online courses or workshops to boost your confidence in making informed financial decisions.

Craft a clear and motivating personal finance vision. Visualise where you want to be financially in 5, 10, or even 20 years. Break down this vision into achievable goals, and outline the steps you need to take to reach each milestone.

Finally, initiate the shift to a positive money mindset by setting small, achievable goals. Whether it's saving a little extra each month, investing in a small-scale project, or simply cutting down on unnecessary expenses, each small victory helps build momentum.

Remember, reshaping your money mindset isn't an overnight

fix but a rewarding journey towards financial freedom. Keep your goals in sight, stay informed, and persistently challenge your old beliefs. Wealth isn't just about having money; it's about having options and the freedom to live on your terms. Let's make it happen!

Notes & Reflections

Fearless Finances

"Do not be embarrassed by your failures, learn from them and start again." - Richard Branson

Identifying Financial Fears

Common Money Fears and Their Origins

Let's kick things off by diving into the deep end of your wallet—figuratively speaking, of course. Money fears, whether you acknowledge them or not, are more common than you might think. Everyone has them at some point, but where do they come from?

Firstly, there's the fear of not having enough. This fear often originates from either past experiences of financial scarcity or societal narratives that equate money with security and success. It's the classic worry that you won't be able to cover your basic needs or that an unexpected expense could sweep the rug from under your feet.

Then, there's the fear of losing what you have. This can stem from witnessing others go through financial hardship, perhaps during economic downturns, or experiencing it firsthand. The volatility of financial markets, or even hearing news of financial disasters, can amplify this fear, making the act of preserving wealth feel like navigating a minefield.

Lastly, the fear of not being capable enough to manage or grow your finances can loom large. This often traces back to a lack of financial education, which isn't typically taught in schools. Many grow up without a clear understanding of how money works, from basic budgeting to investing, leading to a self-doubt about making informed financial decisions.

Understanding the roots of these fears is the first step towards overcoming them. It's about recognising that these fears are not just personal inadequacies but common concerns that you can manage and conquer.

How Fear Limits Financial Growth

Now that we've pinpointed where these fears come from, let's explore how they can put a stranglehold on your financial growth. Fear acts like a barrier. It can paralyse you, keeping you in a state of inaction or pushing you towards overly cautious decisions that hinder wealth accumulation.

For instance, the fear of not having enough might stop you from spending money on opportunities that could lead to growth, such as investing in stocks, furthering your education, or starting a business. It's a defensive strategy—playing not to lose instead of playing to win.

Similarly, the fear of losing money might prevent you from investing in higher-risk, higher-reward opportunities. While it's wise to avoid reckless spending, overly conservative financial strategies often result in missed opportunities. The inflation monster could be munching away at your savings, and you wouldn't even know it until it's too late.

Moreover, if you're afraid of making poor financial decisions due to a lack of knowledge, you might find yourself stuck in analysis paralysis. Overthinking and the inability to make a decision because you fear making the wrong one can cause you to miss out on lucrative ventures that could have been beneficial.

Each of these fears feeds into a cycle of financial stagnation where, instead of growing your wealth, you're merely attempting to safeguard what little you have, potentially leading to regret down the line.

Personal Reflections on Money Anxieties

Reflecting on your own financial fears can be as revealing as it is therapeutic. Think about what keeps you up at night when it comes to your finances. Is it the dread of an empty bank account, the anxiety of debt, or perhaps the pressure to maintain a certain lifestyle?

Understanding your personal relationship with money is crucial. It's about getting to the heart of your financial identity. Are your spending habits driven by necessity, pleasure, or anxiety? Do you view money as a source of security, a means to an end, or a path to happiness?

Consider how these anxieties influence your daily life. Maybe they stop you from pursuing higher-risk job opportunities, or perhaps they push you to underspend, even when investment in yourself could lead to greater earnings in the future.

Taking the time to journal your thoughts can be immensely helpful. Write down what you fear about money and why. Trace these fears back to their origins. Was there a particular event or series of events in your life that shaped your view of money? How do these perceptions affect your financial decisions now?

This exercise isn't just about introspection. It's about setting the stage for overcoming these fears. By acknowledging and understanding your financial anxieties, you equip yourself with the knowledge to face them head-on in the subsequent phases of your financial journey.

Remember, identifying your financial fears isn't about criticising yourself—it's about understanding and managing them to pave the way for a richer, more secure financial future. As you move forward, keep these insights in mind. They are the first step towards transforming your relationship with money and cultivating a mindset that sees beyond the fears to the possibilities ahead.

Overcoming Financial Anxiety

Money, as we're all acutely aware, doesn't just sit quietly in the corner; it demands our constant attention and, often, inflames our deepest anxieties. But let's step back a bit; while financial stress is almost a given in today's complex world, mastering it is not just a possibility but a necessity. Here's how you can turn those financial jitters into a strength rather than a stumbling block.

Techniques for Managing Financial Stress

You've identified your financial fears—now let's tackle them head-on. The first weapon in your arsenal should be a detailed financial plan. This might sound obvious, but you'd be surprised how many people miss this foundational step. Start by charting out your income, expenses, debts, and savings. Knowing exactly where every penny goes not only puts you in control but also reduces that nagging sense of uncertainty.

Next, establish an emergency fund. This is your financial safety net, designed to catch you if you fall. Aim to save at least three to six months' worth of living expenses. The peace of mind that comes from knowing you can handle life's unexpected twists and turns is invaluable and reduces the day-to-day stress over money.

Automation is your friend. Automate your savings, bills, and even investments. This removes the temptation to overspend and ensures your money management stays on track without constant monitoring. Plus, it's one less thing to worry about, freeing up mental space for more creative or productive endeavours.

Finally, educate yourself about money. Financial anxiety often stems from the unknown, so demystify the process. Read books, listen to podcasts, or even consider a financial advisor. Knowledge is power, and the more you understand the financial world, the less intimidating it will seem.

Building Confidence with Money

Confidence with money isn't about how much you have in the bank; it's about how well you manage what you do have. Start small. Set achievable financial goals and celebrate when you reach them. This could be as simple as saving a little extra each month or cutting down on unnecessary expenses. Each victory, no matter how small, builds your financial confidence.

Think of money management as a skill, much like driving. Just as you wouldn't expect to win a Formula One race the first time you get behind the wheel, don't expect to be a financial guru overnight. Give yourself permission to learn and grow without harsh self-judgement. The more you practice, the better you'll get, and the more confident you'll feel.

Another key aspect is to stay proactive. Regularly review your financial plan and adjust as needed. Life changes, and so should your financial strategies. This proactive approach not only improves your financial health but also reinforces your sense of control over your money.

Engage with others about finances. Discussing money has long been a taboo, but open conversations about financial strategies, successes, and even failures can be incredibly enlightening and empowering. You're not alone in your financial journey, and there's much to be learned from the experiences of others.

Role of Mindfulness in Financial Decisions

Mindfulness might seem like a buzzword suited more to yoga than to finance, but incorporating mindful practices into your financial decision-making can profoundly impact your financial health. Start by being fully present when dealing with money matters. This means no multi-tasking. Whether you're paying bills, reviewing your financial statements, or planning investments, give your finances your full attention.

Mindfulness also involves being aware of your emotional state when making financial decisions. Are you buying that expensive gadget because you need it, or are you trying to alleviate feelings of stress or inadequacy? By recognising the emotional impulses that can lead to poor financial choices, you can begin to make decisions that are rational and aligned with your long-term goals.

Lastly, practice gratitude. It's easy to focus on what you don't have. Shift that perspective by regularly acknowledging and appreciating what you do have. This not only fosters a positive mindset but also curbs the impulse for unnecessary spending. Gratitude brings contentment, and contentment leads to smarter financial choices.

By addressing financial stress with a clear, structured plan, building confidence through small, manageable steps, and applying mindfulness to your financial decision-making, you're not just managing your money; you're ensuring it doesn't manage you. Remember, the goal here isn't just to survive financially but to thrive, turning what was once anxiety into assuredness, and ultimately, into an avenue for true financial freedom.

Embracing Risk and Opportunity

Calculated Risk-Taking in Finance

When it comes to wealth creation, the ability to take calibrated risks is a game-changer. You see, every financial decision carries a degree of risk, but not all risks are created equal. Understanding how to weigh the potential benefits against the possible pitfalls is crucial in turning these risks into opportunities.

Firstly, let's demystify the concept of 'calculated risks'. These are not reckless gambles but informed decisions. You start by gathering as much information as possible. This could mean analysing market trends, consulting financial experts, or studying historical data. The goal is to make a decision based on solid evidence rather than a hunch.

For instance, consider investing in the stock market. A calculated risk might involve buying shares in a well-established company when the market dips, knowing that historically, the market has recovered and such companies often bounce back stronger. Here, you're not blindly throwing money at a trendy new stock without research; you're making a strategic move based on historical performance and current market analysis.

Secondly, calculated risk-taking involves setting clear boundaries. Decide in advance how much you're willing to lose and stick to it. This is your risk threshold. It isn't just about mitigating losses but about psychological comfort. Knowing your limits can free you to make decisions without fear.

Finally, embrace diversification. Don't put all your eggs in one basket. Spread your investments across different assets, industries, and even geographies. This strategy reduces risk and can lead to a more robust financial portfolio.

Learning from Financial Mistakes

Every investor, no matter how seasoned, makes mistakes. The key, however, lies not in avoiding mistakes altogether but in leveraging them as powerful learning tools. Each mistake provides valuable insights that can pave the way to future success.

Start by acknowledging and analysing where things went wrong. Did you overestimate a market's potential? Perhaps there was a failure to adequately assess the economic indicators? Or did emotions cloud your judgement? Understanding the root cause of your error is the first step towards preventing similar mistakes.

Next, document your findings. Keep a 'mistake journal'. This might sound tedious, but it's incredibly effective. Write down the details of the decision, why you made it, what went wrong, and how you could do things differently. This record becomes a personal guidebook that you can refer to before making future financial decisions.

Moreover, discuss your experiences with others. Whether it's with a mentor, a financial advisor, or peers in a finance community, conversation can uncover different perspectives and insights that you might not have considered. Often, it's this shared wisdom that leads to better decision-making.

Remember, resilience is key. Don't let fear of failure deter you from taking future risks. Instead, use each mistake as a stepping stone towards a more informed and confident financial future.

Opportunities in Financial Uncertainties

In every economic downturn, in every volatile market, there lies opportunity. While it's natural to feel uncertain during such times, embracing this uncertainty can be your greatest financial strategy.

Firstly, look for undervalued assets. During times of economic stress, assets can often be found at prices below their true value. Real estate during a market crash or quality stocks during a stock market dip are examples. These scenarios provide unique buying opportunities for those with an eye for potential.

Moreover, financial uncertainties often prompt new trends and markets to emerge. The rise of digital currencies and the explosion of e-commerce during recent global crises are testament to this. By staying informed and adaptable, you can be among the first to tap into these emerging opportunities.

It's also a time for innovation. Economic challenges can inspire new business ideas or ways to streamline existing processes in ways that cut costs and boost efficiency. As an investor or entrepreneur, thinking creatively during uncertain times can not only help you survive but thrive.

Lastly, consider the advantages of leveraging technology. Financial technologies, or 'fintech', offer tools that can help navigate financial uncertainties more effectively. From sophisticated trading algorithms to budgeting apps and automated investment advisors, these tools can provide valuable insights and aid in making more informed decisions.

In conclusion, embracing risk is not about being fearless but about being prepared. It's about using knowledge, strategy, and an open mind to turn potential threats into lucrative opportunities. Whether it's through calculated risk-taking, learning from past mistakes, or finding potential in uncertainty, the path to financial freedom involves embracing both risk and opportunity with equal vigour.

Summary and Application Exercises

Congratulations on navigating through the intricacies of Fearless Finances! You've taken a bold step towards understanding and conquering the financial fears that hold many back from true financial freedom. Now, it's time to put this newfound knowledge into practice.

Firstly, reflect on the common money fears you identified and their origins. This awareness is your foundation. Acknowledge these fears but don't allow them to dictate your financial decisions. Remember, understanding where your anxieties stem from is the first step towards overcoming them.

Next, implement the techniques you've learned for managing financial stress. Whether it's setting up an emergency fund, creating a monthly budget, or scheduling regular financial check-ins, these strategies are designed to boost your confidence with money. Confidence is key, as it transforms fear into readiness and capability.

Now, let's talk mindfulness—practice making financial decisions with a clear and present mind. This might mean meditating before reviewing your finances or simply taking a moment to breathe deeply when making significant financial choices. Mindfulness reduces impulsiveness, leading to more thoughtful and successful financial outcomes.

Lastly, embrace risk and opportunity. Start small if you must; it's all about getting comfortable with being uncomfortable. Whether it's investing in stocks, starting a new business venture, or learning a new financial skill, each step is a move towards growth. Remember, every successful financier has taken calculated risks.

Your action steps are clear:

1. Write down your top three financial fears and the reasons behind them

2. Choose one financial stress-reduction technique and practice it weekly

3. Make one mindful financial decision each day, no matter how small

4. Identify a risk you've been avoiding and take a small, calculated step towards it.

By continually practising these steps, you'll not only manage your financial fears but also pave the way towards a richer, more liberated financial life. Here's to your success!

Notes & Reflections

The Habits of Wealth

"WEALTH CONSISTS NOT IN HAVING GREAT POSSESSIONS, BUT IN HAVING FEW WANTS." – EPICTETUS

Daily Practices for Success

In the quest for financial freedom, the devil is truly in the details—or, more precisely, in the daily routines. The first step to cultivating a millionaire mindset isn't found in any high-flying investment strategy; it's in the mundane, day-to-day habits that pave the way for long-term wealth accumulation. Let's break down these daily practices into three actionable parts: structuring your day for financial success, wealth-building routines, and the power of consistency.

Structuring Your Day for Financial Success

Imagine your day as a blank canvas. How you fill that canvas directs not only how you spend your hours, but also how effectively you can build your wealth. Start with the basics: prioritise your tasks. What you do first thing in the morning sets the tone for the rest of your day. Consider beginning with a task that aligns closely with your financial goals. It could be as simple as reviewing your financial goals, checking your investments, or reading up on market news over breakfast.

Time-blocking is a powerful technique here. Divide your day into blocks dedicated solely to specific activities, including those related to managing and growing your wealth. For instance, you might reserve your early mornings for strategic financial planning, leaving afternoons free for execution and evenings for education and reflection.

Remember, the key to structuring your day effectively lies in recognizing your personal peak productivity periods. Are you a morning person, or do you find your stride after lunch? Align your most challenging financial tasks with these peak times to maximise your effectiveness.

Wealth-Building Routines

Building wealth isn't a one-off event but a habit. Here, we explore routines that can turn your everyday into a wealth-building powerhouse. First off, make it a routine to set clear, measurable financial objectives. Whether it's increasing your savings rate by 1% every month or investing £200 in stocks bi-weekly, these targets should guide your daily actions.

Automation plays a critical role in wealth-building routines. Automate your savings and investments to ensure they happen without fail. This removes the temptation to skip a month and helps inculcate a 'pay yourself first' mentality. Every pay period, have a portion of your earnings automatically transferred to your savings or investment accounts before you have a chance to spend it.

Moreover, keep your financial knowledge sharp. Dedicate at least 15 minutes of your day to learning about personal finance and investment strategies. This could involve listening to a finance podcast, reading a chapter from a financial book, or even scrolling through financial news. Over time, this knowledge builds up, equipping you with the tools to make smarter financial decisions.

The Power of Consistency

Consistency is the glue that holds your financial strategies together. It's one thing to start a routine, quite another to stick to it. The most successful financial moguls aren't necessarily those with the best strategies, but those who apply good strategies consistently over time.

Maintain a daily journal of your financial actions. This might seem tedious, but it's incredibly effective for maintaining consistency. Each day, jot down what you did towards achieving your financial goals. Did you stick to your budget? How did you handle financial temptations or emergencies? Reflecting on this daily can reinforce good habits and help you see patterns in your behaviour that require adjustment.

Moreover, consistency in your financial life should also mean a consistent review and adjustment of your strategies. As your financial situation evolves, so too should your routines and strategies. Allocate a time each week or month to review your financial progress against your goals. This isn't just about patting yourself on the back for a job well done—it's about critically assessing what's working and what isn't and making necessary adjustments.

In conclusion, remember that financial freedom isn't just about making money; it's about making smart choices consistently. Start embedding these daily practices into your routine, and you'll be on your way to a richer life in no time. Keep at it, and let these routines be the foundation upon which your financial empire is built.

Smart Money Management

Budgeting Effectively

Budgeting effectively is less about restriction and more about understanding where your treasure trove is being allocated. Imagine you're the captain of a ship. Your funds are the wind in your sails, and budgeting is your map. Without this map, you're simply floating on the ocean hoping to stumble upon treasure. To begin, you need to look at what you earn versus what you spend, categorise your expenses, and then set targets that make sense not just for surviving, but for thriving.

The first step is tracking. For a month, keep a detailed record of where every pound is going. This includes every coffee, every impulse buy, every seemingly insignificant amount. You might feel it's tedious, but this is the groundwork of successful financial management. Once you've got a clear picture, categorise these into essentials and non-essentials. Essentials include rent, utilities, groceries, and transport, while non-essentials could be dining out, subscriptions, and miscellaneous purchases.

Now, create a budget that helps you achieve your financial goals. Allocate a percentage of your income to your essentials, savings, investments, and some for leisure. A popular method is the 50/30/20 rule, where 50% of your income goes to necessities, 30% to wants, and 20% to savings and investments. Adjust these percentages based on your personal goals and financial situation.

Saving v Investing

Next, let's talk about saving versus investing. Both are crucial, yet serve different purposes. Saving is your financial safety net. It's immediate, accessible, and low-risk. This is the money you stash away for sudden medical expenses, car repairs, or that unexpected job loss. Ideally, aim to have at least three to six months' worth of living expenses in a high-interest savings account where your money can grow, but remains accessible.

Investing, on the other hand, is your wealth builder. It carries more risk but offers greater return potential. You're putting your money into stocks, bonds, mutual funds, real estate, or other assets with the expectation that over time, they will increase in value. Think of investing as planting a garden. It takes time, patience, and a bit of risk. You water it (invest more money), weed it (adjust your portfolio as needed), and eventually, it grows and bears fruit (returns).

It's crucial to understand your risk tolerance and diversify your investments. Don't put all your eggs in one basket. Spread your investments across different asset classes to mitigate risk and maximise potential returns. For instance, while stocks may offer high returns, they are also more volatile. Bonds, on the other hand, are generally safer but offer lower returns. A balanced portfolio reduces risk and can help you achieve steady growth.

Tools & Apps for Financial Tracking

Finally, technology has made managing finances significantly easier. There are numerous tools and apps designed to help you track your spending, budget, save, and invest. Apps like Mint or YNAB (You Need A Budget) can connect to your bank account and categorise your spending for you, helping you stick to your budget. Investment apps like Nutmeg or Moneybox can help simplify the investment process by automating investments based on your risk profile and financial goals.

For those who find budgeting challenging, these apps can be lifesavers. They provide insights into your financial habits and help you see the bigger picture. Plus, many offer educational resources to improve your financial literacy, empowering you to make smarter financial decisions.

Understanding and managing your money effectively is a pivotal skill in building wealth. By budgeting effectively, balancing saving and investing, and leveraging financial tools, you're setting the stage for financial success. Remember, smart money management isn't about pinching pennies; it's about making every penny work for you. As you continue to refine these practices, you'll find that managing your finances becomes less stressful and more strategic, paving the way for a richer life both materially and experientially. So, take charge of your financial ship and steer it towards the treasure you deserve.

Long-Term Financial Strategies

Retirement Planning

Picture this: you, in your late 60s or perhaps early 70s, sipping something delightful on a beach or crafting the next great novel in your cosy study. Sounds like a dream? Well, it's time to turn that dream into a plan with astute retirement planning. It's never too early or too late to start thinking about retirement. However, the earlier you start, the more comfortable and stress-free your retirement can be.

First and foremost, get to grips with the basics of pension schemes available to you. Whether it's an employer-sponsored pension plan, such as a workplace pension, or a personal pension like a SIPP (Self-Invested Personal Pension), each has its own benefits and rules. Understanding these will allow you to maximise the contributions and tax advantages they offer.

Next, consider how much you'll need to retire comfortably. This isn't about pulling a random number out of the air—it's about calculating your expected living costs in retirement, factoring in inflation, and planning for unforeseen expenses that might pop up. Online calculators can be a good starting point, but it might be wise to consult a financial advisor to help tailor a plan specific to your needs and goals.

Once you've set a target, it's time to strategise how to reach it. This includes deciding on your investment strategy. Diversification is key here. A mix of equities, bonds, and other assets can help balance risk and return. Remember, retirement planning is a marathon, not a sprint. Regular reviews of your plan can help ensure you remain on track to meet your goals despite the market's ups and downs.

Diversifying Income Streams

Relying solely on your day job for income can be akin to putting all your eggs in one basket. Diversifying your income streams can not only accelerate your path to financial freedom but also provide an added security layer in troubled times.

Start by exploring side hustles that align with your skills or passions. This could be anything from freelance writing or web design to selling handmade goods online. The key here is to find something that you are passionate about, so it doesn't just feel like another job but rather an enjoyable and profitable venture.

Property investment is another popular way to diversify income. Whether it's buying to let or investing in real estate investment trusts (REITs), property can provide a steady stream of passive income alongside capital appreciation over the long term. However, it's important to do your due diligence and understand the market conditions, as well as any potential risks involved.

Lastly, think about investing in financial markets. This could be through stocks, bonds, mutual funds, or even newer areas like cryptocurrencies. Each comes with its own set of risks and rewards, so it's crucial to educate yourself or consult a professional to craft a portfolio that matches your risk tolerance and financial goals.

Planning for Financial Milestones

Life is full of milestones: buying a home, sending your kids to university, or even starting your own business. Planning for these financial milestones is crucial because it not only ensures that you are prepared when they arrive but also helps prevent them from derailing your long-term financial well-being.

Start by identifying the major expenses you expect to encounter in the future. Once you have a clear idea, set up dedicated savings pots for each milestone. This could be through regular savings accounts, ISAs, or even specific investment accounts designed for long-term goals. Automating your savings can make this process easier and help keep you disciplined about contributing regularly.

For each milestone, consider the most efficient way to finance it. For instance, if you're saving for a child's education, explore options like education savings accounts that offer tax advantages. If you're buying a property, look into different types of mortgages and government schemes that might be available to you.

Lastly, always have a contingency plan. Life can be unpredictable, and having an emergency fund or insurance in place can help you manage any financial surprises without sacrificing your long-term goals.

By taking a proactive approach to retirement planning, diversifying your income streams, and planning for significant financial milestones, you can build a robust financial foundation that not only meets your needs today but also secures your financial freedom for the future. Each step you take brings you closer to a rich life, not just in monetary terms but in quality and satisfaction. Remember, the journey to financial freedom isn't just about the destination but also about making wise choices along the way.

Summary & Application Exercises

Congratulations on completing the chapter on The Habits of Wealth. By now, you should have a toolkit brimming with strategies to enhance your financial health, from daily routines that pave the way to success, to smart money management, right through to planning for the long term.

Firstly, reflect on your daily practices. Have you structured your day to maximise financial success? Remember, consistency is your ally. Incorporate those wealth-building routines into your day, whether it's reviewing your financial goals each morning or setting aside time weekly to analyse your spending.

Now, let's talk about managing your money wisely. If you

haven't already set up a budget, make that your priority. It's the compass that will guide your financial decisions. Experiment with different tools and apps to find which one best helps you track your spending and investments. This will make budgeting and managing your finances an easier and more accurate process.

Investing is not just saving on steroids; it's a way to make your money work for you. Evaluate the balance between saving and investing. Start small if you're new to investing, but start. The key is to get into the habit of making your money grow.

Looking ahead, consider your long-term financial health. Have you started planning for retirement? Are you diversifying your income streams? These aren't just tasks for the future; they're tasks for now. Begin by setting clear financial milestones and mapping out a plan to achieve them.

Here's your action plan:

1. Review and refine your daily financial routines every month

2. Set up a budget using a digital tool that suits your needs, and stick to it

3. Allocate funds to both savings and investments regularly

4. Start planning for retirement now, not later

5. Identify potential new income streams every six months.

Remember, wealth isn't built in a day. It's the product of daily habits, smart management, and long-term strategies. Stick to the plan, stay consistent, and watch as your financial life transforms, paving the way to a richer life. Go ahead, take control of your financial destiny—step by step, day by day.

Notes & Reflections

Income Acceleration

"The only limit to our realisation of tomorrow will be our doubts of today." - Franklin D. Roosevelt

Increasing Your Earning Potential

In the quest for financial freedom, increasing your earning potential is a crucial step. Think of it as building a powerful engine in your wealth-creation vehicle. It's not just about working harder, but smarter. Let's explore how you can amplify your income through three effective strategies: enhancing your skills and education, negotiating better salaries and raises, and diving into the lucrative world of side hustles and passive income.

Skills and Education

In today's fast-paced world, the thirst for knowledge is never quenched. Continuous learning isn't just a nice-to-have, it's a must if you want to stay ahead. But where do you begin? Focus on skills that are in high demand and align with your interests. Technology skills, like coding or digital marketing, are universally beneficial and often self-taught through online platforms such as Coursera or Udemy. These platforms offer courses created by top-notch universities and companies, making it easier for you to get quality education at a fraction of the cost.

However, don't just limit yourself to hard skills. Soft skills, such as leadership, communication, and critical thinking, are equally important. These can elevate your appeal in any job market. Consider workshops, mentoring, and reading as ways to develop these skills. Books like "How to Win Friends and Influence People" by Dale Carnegie can be a great start.

Another tip is to always be in the know. Subscribe to industry newsletters, follow thought leaders on social media, and participate in relevant webinars and conferences. This not only broadens your perspective but also enhances your network, often leading to unexpected opportunities.

Negotiating Salaries and Raises

Negotiation is an art, and when it comes to your salary, it's an art worth mastering. Start by understanding your worth. Tools like Glassdoor and Payscale can provide insights into what others in your field and region are earning. Armed with this information, you can negotiate from a position of strength.

Preparation is key. Before entering a negotiation, list your recent achievements, especially those that have positively impacted the bottom line. Be ready to discuss these accomplishments in a way that highlights your value to the company.

Timing is also crucial. A good time to negotiate might be during a performance review or after the successful completion of a significant project. Approach the conversation with confidence but remain flexible and open to counteroffers, which might include benefits or other compensation if a raise isn't feasible at the moment.

Remember, negotiation is a two-way street. Understand the needs and constraints of your employer and propose solutions that benefit both parties. This not only increases the likelihood of a successful negotiation but also positions you as a strategic thinker.

Side Hustles and Passive Income Ideas

In the age of the gig economy, side hustles are more than just a way to make extra cash; they are potential pathways to significant financial growth. The key is to find a side hustle that you can be passionate about, one that can eventually be automated or require minimal ongoing effort.

For starters, consider leveraging your existing skills. If you're a graphic designer by day, freelance projects can be a lucrative side hustle. Platforms like Upwork and Fiverr make it easier to find freelance gigs. Alternatively, if you have a spare room, platforms like Airbnb can turn it into a passive income source.

Technology also offers new avenues for passive income. Creating an app or a website can provide continuous revenue through ads or subscriptions. If technology isn't your forte, think about low-entry investment opportunities like print-on-demand services or dropshipping, which eliminate the need for inventory and can be managed from your laptop.

Investing in your education around these areas is crucial. Numerous online courses offer insights into setting up and scaling these businesses, so invest some time in learning the ropes before diving in.

In conclusion, increasing your earning potential is a multifaceted approach that involves advancing your education, honing your negotiation skills, and exploring entrepreneurial ventures on the side. Each step you take not only brings you closer to financial freedom but also empowers you to lead a richer, more fulfilling life. So, start today, and remember, the path to financial success is always under construction. Keep paving your way forward with new skills, bold negotiations, and innovative side hustles.

Entrepreneurial Mindset

Finding Business Opportunities

In the world of entrepreneurship, spotting the right business opportunity is akin to finding a needle in a haystack. It's not merely about what you know; it's significantly about how you think and perceive the world around you. The key is to cultivate a mindset that consistently seeks gaps in markets, inefficiencies in processes, and unmet needs within consumer bases.

Firstly, become a trend-spotter. This involves staying updated with emerging trends in technology, consumer behaviour, and global economic shifts. It's crucial to look beyond the obvious and predictable; delve into niche markets where there is less competition but a growing interest. For instance, the recent surge in plant-based products wasn't just about dietary choices; it was a response to deeper values regarding health, ethics, and sustainability.

Secondly, use problems as your guide. Every problem you encounter is a potential business opportunity. Whether it's something that frustrates you personally or a challenge that you notice others struggling with, these are golden opportunities for innovation. For example, the frustration with the inefficiency of traditional banks led to the fintech revolution. Tools like Revolut and Monzo didn't just happen; they were born out of real-world frustrations.

Lastly, listen and observe. Your next great business idea could come from a casual conversation at a coffee shop or while observing the hustle and bustle of city life. Pay attention to what people complain about, what they wish they had, and what makes their lives easier. These insights are invaluable when brainstorming business ideas.

The Basics of Starting a Business

Once you've identified a promising opportunity, the real work begins: starting your business. This can seem daunting, but breaking it down into manageable steps can simplify the process.

First and foremost, validate your idea. Before you dive into the deep end, it's crucial to test the waters. This could be as simple as discussing your idea with potential customers or as structured as creating a minimum viable product (MVP) to gauge interest. Tools like surveys, focus groups, and beta testing can provide essential feedback that can shape your concept into something the market truly desires.

Next, focus on the legal and administrative framework. Registering your business, understanding tax obligations, and securing any necessary licenses can be tedious but are absolutely essential. It's also wise to familiarize yourself with the basics of contracting if your business requires you to enter into agreements with other parties.

Then, plan your finances. Start-up costs can vary widely depending on your business model, but every entrepreneur needs a clear financial plan. This includes budgeting for initial expenses, forecasting revenue, and planning for contingencies. Tools like Excel or Google Sheets are great for financial planning, but consider software like QuickBooks or Xero as your business grows.

Additionally, develop a robust marketing strategy. In today's digital age, this often involves building a strong online presence through a professional website, active social media accounts, and perhaps an SEO-optimised blog. Offline methods, though sometimes overlooked, such as networking events, can also be incredibly powerful.

Learning from Successful Entrepreneurs

Finally, one of the most invaluable resources at your disposal is the wisdom of those who've already travelled the road you're embarking on. Learning from successful entrepreneurs can accelerate your journey and help you avoid common pitfalls.

Start by identifying entrepreneurs within and outside your industry whose success stories inspire you. What paths did they take? What mistakes did they make? What unique strategies did they employ? Books, podcasts, and interviews are great resources for gaining insights into their experiences.

Consider the power of mentorship. Engaging directly with a mentor can provide you with personalised guidance and support. This doesn't necessarily mean hiring a high-profile coach. Many successful entrepreneurs are willing to share their knowledge through mentoring programmes or even informal chats. Don't be afraid to reach out — you'd be surprised how receptive many are to helping newcomers.

Moreover, analyse their failures as much as their successes. Every entrepreneur faces setbacks, but it's how they respond to these hurdles that often dictates their level of success. Understand that failure is not the opposite of success; it's part of the success story.

In conclusion, adopting an entrepreneurial mindset isn't just about launching a business; it's about seeing the world as a playground of potential. With the right approach to finding opportunities, the basics of setting up your business, and learning from those who have succeeded, you are well on your way to crafting not just a business, but a lifestyle that aligns with your aspirations for financial freedom. Embrace the journey, for it is as rewarding as the destination itself.

Investments and Assets

Basics of Investing

When you're starting to think about investing, it's like learning to drive. There's a bit of theory, sure, but the real learning happens when you get behind the wheel. The road to financial freedom isn't paved with intentions; it's built with investments. Let's break down the essentials.

First up, understand your risk tolerance. Everyone has a different comfort level with risk. Some of us are skydivers; others aren't keen on roller coasters. Knowing where you stand can help you decide how to allocate your investments. Think of it as deciding whether you're more of a 'fast and furious' or 'slow and steady wins the race' kind of investor.

Next, diversification is your best friend. Don't put all your eggs in one basket. Spread your investments across different asset classes (like stocks, bonds, and real estate) and within those classes. This helps manage risk and reduce the impact of any single investment performing poorly.

Lastly, understand the power of compound interest. It's the secret sauce of investing. Compound interest occurs when the interest that accrues on an investment is reinvested to generate additional earnings over time. It's like rolling a snowball down a hill; it starts small but can grow significantly over time. Albert Einstein reportedly called compound interest "the eighth wonder of the world", and who are we to argue with Einstein?

Real Estate

Transitioning to real estate, it's often seen as a rite of passage on the journey to wealth. The allure is clear: it's tangible, it can provide passive income, and it often appreciates in value. But like any investment, it comes with its own set of rules.

First, understand the market. Real estate isn't just about buying a house. It's about understanding local market trends, economic factors, and what drives demand in specific areas. Are you looking into an up-and-coming neighbourhood, or is it a well-established one? Each has its strategies and risks.

Then there's the matter of leverage. In real estate, you can use a relatively small amount of your own money to secure a much larger asset. This is because real estate investments are typically made with a mortgage. While leverage can amplify your returns, remember it can also increase your losses, so handle with care.

Think about cash flow. If you're buying to let, your goal should be to have your rental income exceed your expenses, including mortgage payments, maintenance, and taxes. Positive cash flow is king because it means the investment is putting money in your pocket regularly, beyond just the potential for property appreciation.

Stocks and Bonds

Moving onto stocks and bonds, these are the bread and butter of many investment portfolios. Stocks allow you to own a slice of a company, and ideally, as the company grows, so does the value of your slice. Bonds, on the other hand, are more like giving a loan to a company or government, and in return, you get regular interest payments.

With stocks, the key is to think long-term. Stock markets can be volatile, swinging up and down on daily news, but history shows that over years and decades, they tend to grow. Investing in a mix of individual stocks and stock mutual funds can help spread out your risk.

For bonds, it's all about the ratings. Bonds are graded based on the creditworthiness of the issuer. Higher ratings, like AAA, indicate lower risk but also lower returns. Lower ratings are riskier, but they offer higher returns. Balancing risk and return is crucial.

Alternative Investments like Cryptocurrencies

Finally, let's touch on alternative investments, focusing on cryptocurrencies like Bitcoin and Ethereum. These digital assets represent a frontier in investing, far removed from traditional realms like stocks and bonds.

Cryptocurrencies are highly volatile. Prices can skyrocket, then plummet, within days or even hours. This makes them risky, but for some, the potential high rewards are worth it. Before diving in, educate yourself. Understand what drives cryptocurrency markets, such as investor sentiment, market demand, technological developments, and regulatory news.

Using cryptocurrencies also means getting familiar with new technologies like blockchain and digital wallets. Security is paramount because, unlike traditional banks, there's no safety net if things go wrong.

In conclusion, whether it's building a portfolio of stocks and bonds, renting out properties, or speculating on cryptocurrency, each asset class comes with its own set of challenges and opportunities. The key is to start, learn continuously, and adjust your strategy as you gain more insight. Welcome to the dynamic world of investments, where the rules of the game are yours to master.

Summary & Application Exercises

Congratulations on making it through the deep dive into Income Acceleration! You've now armed yourself with critical strategies to increase your earning potential, adopt an entrepreneurial mindset, and make savvy investment choices.

Let's take a moment to summarise and then leap into action. Firstly, boosting your earning potential isn't just about hard work; it's about smart work. Enhancing your skills and education, mastering the art of negotiation for salaries and raises, and exploring side hustles or passive income streams are foundational steps. Remember, every skill you learn not only adds to your value but also opens up new avenues for income.

Next, fostering an entrepreneurial mindset is about seeing opportunities where others see obstacles. It involves understanding the nuts and bolts of starting a business and drawing inspiration from established entrepreneurs. This mindset isn't confined to starting a business; it's about thinking like an entrepreneur in every aspect of your life.

Lastly, in investments and assets, we've touched on everything from the basics of investing to specific areas like real estate, stocks, bonds, and even alternative options like cryptocurrencies. Diversifying your investment portfolio is crucial to mitigating risks and maximising returns.

Now, for the action items:

1. **Skill Enhancement:** Identify one skill relevant to your field that you can improve or a new skill you can acquire. Look for online courses, workshops, or books that can help you in this quest.

2. **Negotiation Practice:** Prepare for your next salary negotiation by researching average pay scales for your role and industry. Practice your negotiation strategies with a friend or mentor.

3. **Explore Side Hustles:** List out five potential side hustles. Evaluate each based on your interests, time availability, and initial investment required. Choose one to start within the next month.

4. **Opportunity Identification:** Keep a journal of business ideas and opportunities you observe in your daily life. Review this journal weekly to refine your ideas and assess feasibility.

5. **Learn from Leaders:** Pick an entrepreneur you admire and study their career. Identify three key business strategies they used and consider how you can apply them in your own ventures.

6. **Investment Research:** Allocate time each week to research investment opportunities. Start with one asset class you are less familiar with to broaden your understanding.

7. **Financial Review:** Schedule a monthly financial review to assess your income streams, track spending, and review investment performance. Adjust as needed to stay on target for your financial goals.

By integrating these practices into your life, you're not just dreaming of financial freedom; you're actively constructing it.

You've just navigated through a treasure trove of strategies designed to put your income on the fast track. Now, it's time to capitalise on this newfound knowledge and shift into high gear towards your financial freedom.

Starting with your earning potential, remember that investing in skills and education is not just about climbing the corporate ladder; it's about equipping yourself with the tools to thrive in any economic climate. Take action by identifying skills that are in high demand within your industry and seek out courses or training that can help you master them. Next, harness the power of negotiation. Approach your next salary discussion with confidence, armed with data on industry standards and a clear articulation of your accomplishments. Lastly, diversify your income streams. Whether it's a side hustle or exploring passive income opportunities, start small. Even a modest additional income can snowball over time.

Switching gears to an entrepreneurial mindset, begin by staying curious and observant. Opportunities are often disguised as problems waiting for a solution. Write down any inefficiencies or gaps you notice in your daily life and brainstorm possible business ideas that could address them. When you're ready to take the plunge into starting a business, focus on the basics: create a solid business plan, understand your market, and don't shy away from seeking advice from those who have walked this path before.

Finally, let's talk about investments and assets. Begin with the basics of investing; understand different investment vehicles and find the ones that align with your risk tolerance and financial goals. Real estate and stocks and bonds are traditional paths worth exploring, but don't ignore the burgeoning field of alternative investments, including cryptocurrencies. However, ensure you do your due diligence and research thoroughly before diving in.

Your journey to financial freedom is a marathon, not a sprint. Set realistic goals, take calculated risks, and stay informed. The road ahead is paved with opportunities; you just need to take that first step. Start today by choosing one action item from each section and commit to it. Remember, the best time to plant a tree was 20 years ago. The second best time is now.

Notes & Reflections

Breaking Free From Debt

"The borrower is servant to the lender." - Proverbs 22:7

Understanding Debt

Grasping the true nature of debt is like unlocking the first door on your path to financial liberation. Let's dive in and dismantle some of the complexities surrounding this often intimidating subject.

Types of Debt

First off, not all debt is created equal. You've likely heard terms like 'good debt' and 'bad debt' tossed around, but what do they really mean? Let's clarify.

Good debt is typically associated with borrowing that can increase your net worth or has future value. Think mortgages or student loans. Yes, they're hefty commitments, but they're investments in your future; assets that might appreciate over time or increase your earning potential.

On the other hand, **bad debt** usually involves purchases that depreciate quickly and don't contribute to your financial growth. Credit card debt is a classic example. It's easy to accumulate, carries high interest rates, and often finances items that lose value rapidly.

Understanding these distinctions is crucial because it influences how you manage and prioritise your debts, which we'll touch on later.

How Debt Affects Financial Freedom

Debt can be a massive barrier in your quest for financial freedom. It's like trying to fill a leaking bucket, isn't it? You keep pouring money in, but if you're not careful, interest payments and fees can drain your resources faster than you can fill it.

Here's a clearer picture: imagine your income is a pie. Every slice represents a financial commitment. The more debt you have, the fewer slices remain for savings, investment, and spending on experiences or items that bring you joy. High levels of debt can mean smaller and fewer slices, which can significantly restrict your financial flexibility.

Moreover, debt often comes with emotional weight. The stress of mounting bills can affect your mental health and overall well-being, making it harder to make wise financial decisions. It's a vicious cycle: stress leads to poor decisions, which lead to more debt. Breaking this cycle by managing debt effectively is a step towards regaining control of your financial life.

Strategies for Managing Debt

Managing debt needn't be a Herculean task. With the right strategies, you can navigate through it more smoothly than you might think.

Understand What You Owe: Start by laying all your cards on the table. List out each debt, including the creditor, total amount owed, interest rate, and monthly payment. This gives you a complete picture of what you're dealing with.

Create a Budget: It sounds basic because it is – basic but powerful. Knowing exactly what you earn and spend each month is crucial. It helps you find opportunities to cut back and allocate more funds toward debt repayment.

Use the Avalanche or Snowball Method: These are two popular strategies for paying off debt. The avalanche method involves paying off debts with the highest interest rates first, which saves you money on interest over time. The snowball method, on the other hand, focuses on paying off smaller debts first, providing psychological wins that can motivate you to keep going.

Consider Consolidation: If you're juggling multiple debts, consolidation might be a viable strategy. This involves taking out a new loan to pay off a variety of debts, leaving you with just one monthly payment. Often, the new loan will have a lower interest rate, making it easier and quicker to pay down your debt.

Stay Informed: Interest rates and financial products are constantly changing. Staying informed can help you make decisions that might benefit your specific situation, such as deciding to refinance a high-interest loan when rates drop.

Managing debt is not just about paying off what you owe. It's about understanding the landscape, planning your route, and using the right tools to navigate your journey. With each step you take, you move closer to the freedom of a life less burdened by financial constraints.

By tackling the understanding of debt head-on, recognising how it operates and impacts your life, and strategically managing your liabilities, you're laying down a robust foundation for your financial house. Remember, every journey begins with understanding where you stand. Now that you're equipped with this knowledge, you're ready to take the next steps towards not just managing your debt, but mastering it.

Strategies to Reduce Debt

In the world of personal finance, knowledge is power, and action is king. Now that you've got a deeper understanding of debt and its impact on your financial freedom, it's time to roll up your sleeves and get proactive about reducing your debt. Let's dive into some strategies that can help you not only chip away at what you owe but also reclaim your financial independence.

Debt Repayment Methods

Different strokes for different folks — the same applies to debt repayment. There are numerous methods out there, but two popular strategies stand out: the Snowball Method and the Avalanche Method. Each has its merits, depending on your personal financial situation and psychological makeup.

The Snowball Method is particularly effective if you're someone who needs to see quick results to stay motivated. Here's how it works: you list all your debts from the smallest to the largest amount. You make minimum payments on all your debts except for the smallest one, which you target with as much money as you can muster. Once that's paid off, you take the money you were putting toward that debt and add it to the minimum payment on the next smallest debt, and so forth. The process creates a 'snowball effect' as your free cash flow grows and gets thrown onto larger debts, knocking them out one by one.

On the other hand, **the Avalanche Method** might appeal to the number crunchers. This approach involves paying off debts with the highest interest rates first while making minimum payments on others. It might not give you the quick wins of the Snowball Method, but it's cost-effective. By clearing high-interest debts first, you reduce the amount of interest you pay over time, which can be significant depending on the sizes and rates of your debts.

Prioritising Debts

When you're trying to dig yourself out of a financial hole, not all debts are created equal. Prioritising them can significantly affect how quickly you can become debt-free and how much interest you pay in the long run. Here's a quick guide on how to tackle this:

1. **Secure vs Unsecured:** Start with unsecured debts such as credit cards and personal loans. These typically have higher interest rates than secured debts like mortgages or car loans and can balloon quickly

2. **Interest Rates:** As mentioned earlier, you should also consider the interest rates. Debts with higher rates are costlier, so they often deserve priority as they eat up more of your resources over time

3. **Consequences of Non-Payment:** Think about the implications of not keeping up with payments. For instance, failing to

pay your mortgage could cost you your home, so it's crucial to keep those payments up even if you're focusing extra payments elsewhere.

By assessing which debts affect your financial health most severely, you can tailor your repayment strategy to be as efficient and effective as possible.

When to Seek Professional Help

There's no shame in seeking help; in fact, recognising when you need professional advice is a hallmark of savvy financial thinking. If you find yourself overwhelmed by your debt, or if your efforts to manage it aren't yielding results, it might be time to call in the experts.

Credit Counselling: A good first step could be to consult with a credit counsellor. These professionals can provide valuable advice on managing your debts, help negotiate with creditors, and potentially set up a Debt Management Plan (DMP) tailored for you. A DMP can help reduce your interest rates or monthly payments and give you a clear timeline for paying off your debts.

Debt Consolidation: Another option might be debt consolidation, where you combine multiple debts into a single debt, often with a lower interest rate. This can simplify your finances and make debts easier to manage. However, it's crucial to crunch the numbers and possibly consult a financial advisor to ensure this really is the best option for you.

Insolvency Practitioners: In severe cases, where other debt reduction strategies are not viable, consulting with an insolvency practitioner could be the next step. Solutions like an Individual Voluntary Arrangement (IVA) or even bankruptcy could provide a way out. These are serious steps that require professional guidance and should only be considered as last resorts.

Reducing debt isn't just about improving your balance sheet; it's about setting the stage for a richer, more secure life. By understanding and using these strategies effectively, you're not just getting rid of debt; you're investing in your financial future. So, take a deep breath, choose your strategy, and start your journey towards a life where you call the shots, not your debts.

Living Debt-Free

Building an Emergency Fund

Imagine this: you're finally debt-free. The shackles are off, and the horizon looks incredibly inviting. But before you embark on this new journey of financial freedom, there's an essential first step you need to take – building an emergency fund. Think of it as your financial safety net, designed to catch you if ever you stumble again.

An emergency fund is essentially a buffer of money, set aside to cover unexpected expenses, such as a medical emergency, urgent car repairs, or sudden job loss. The aim here is to prevent these unforeseen events from pushing you back into debt. So, how much should you save? A good rule of thumb is to aim for three to six months' worth of living expenses. This might sound daunting, but the peace of mind it brings is absolutely worth every penny.

To start, open a dedicated savings account for your emergency fund – this separates your fund from your regular spending. Make your contributions automatic, perhaps by setting up a direct debit that transfers a fixed sum from your main account each month. Even small amounts can snowball over time, thanks to the magic of compound interest.

Remember, the goal is consistency, not speed. Even if you're only able to stash away a small percentage of your income, it's still progress. And once you've built up your emergency fund, you'll find that this financial buffer not only provides security but also empowers you to make decisions with greater confidence and less stress.

The Psychological Benefits of Being Debt-Free

Now, let's talk about the less tangible, but incredibly significant benefits of living debt-free – the psychological advantages. Freeing yourself from debt does more than just improve your financial situation; it profoundly impacts your mental and emotional health.

Firstly, consider the reduction in stress. Debt is often accompanied by constant worry about keeping up with payments and the fear of what might happen if you don't. Once debt is out of the picture, this stress dissipates. You're no longer weighed down by financial burdens, which means you can sleep better at night, your relationships can improve, and your general wellbeing can flourish.

Moreover, being debt-free enhances your sense of freedom. You now have the liberty to make choices based on what you truly want or need, rather than being dictated by financial constraints. Want to switch careers, start a business, or take a sabbatical? These options become much more accessible when you aren't servicing debt.

There's also a significant boost in self-esteem that comes with conquering debt. It's a monumental achievement and one that can change the way you view yourself and your abilities. This newfound confidence can spill over into other areas of your life, pushing you to set and achieve new goals that you might have previously thought were out of reach.

Maintaining a Debt-Free Lifestyle

So, you've cleared your debts, built your emergency fund, and are reaping the psychological rewards of being debt-free. The final piece of the puzzle is ensuring you maintain this liberating lifestyle. Here are some strategies to help you stay on track.

First and foremost, continue to live within your means. This is the golden rule of personal finance. Avoid the temptation to inflate your lifestyle just because you have more disposable income. Instead, focus on increasing your savings and investments. This doesn't mean you can't enjoy your money, but it does mean making thoughtful decisions about spending.

Create a budget and stick to it. Yes, the dreaded 'B' word. But in reality, a budget is just a plan for your money, ensuring that you're spending it in ways that reflect your priorities and goals. Regularly review and adjust your budget to fit your current circumstances and future aspirations.

Moreover, stay vigilant against accumulating new debt. This might mean saying no to high-limit credit cards or flashy car loans. If you do decide to take on debt (like a mortgage), ensure it's manageable and aligns with your long-term financial goals.

Lastly, continue educating yourself about money management. The world of finance is always evolving, and staying informed will help you make smarter financial decisions. Whether it's reading books, listening to podcasts, or even attending workshops, ongoing education is key to maintaining financial freedom.

Living debt-free is not just about enjoying your current financial situation but also securing your financial future. By building an emergency fund, acknowledging the psychological benefits, and adopting strategies to maintain a debt-free life, you're not just surviving without debt – you're thriving. And in this newfound financial landscape, the possibilities are truly endless. Embrace it, enjoy it, and most importantly, protect it.

Summary & Application Exercises

Congratulations on completing this crucial chapter on Breaking Free From Debt. You've equipped yourself with the understanding of different types of debt, the impact they have on your journey to financial freedom, and the strategies needed to manage and reduce them. Now, let's make sure that freedom becomes a reality.

Step1: Assess Your Debt Start by listing all your debts. Include everything from credit card balances to loans and mortgages. Understanding the full scope of what you owe is the first step towards managing it effectively.

Step 2: Create a Debt Reduction Plan Using the strategies discussed, such as the debt snowball or avalanche method, set up a plan that prioritises your debts in a way that makes sense for your financial situation. Stick to the plan by making consistent payments, and adjust as needed to prevent new debts from accumulating.

Step 3: Establish an Emergency Fund Begin to set aside a small portion of your income into an emergency fund. Aim for an initial target that could cover at least one month of living expenses, and gradually increase it. This fund is crucial for avoiding new debts in the face of unexpected expenses.

Step 4: Embrace the Psychological Shift Recognise and celebrate the mental relief and freedom that comes from reducing debt. Let this positive change reinforce your commitment to a debt-free lifestyle.

Step 5: Maintain Your Debt-Free Lifestyle Continue to live within your means, avoid accumulating new debt, and keep saving. Regularly review your financial habits and adjust your budget as necessary to ensure you stay on track.

Remember, breaking free from debt is not just about adjusting your finances, it's about transforming your life. Each step you take builds a foundation for lasting financial health and freedom. Stick with it, and enjoy the rich life that comes from being in control of your financial destiny.

Notes & Reflections

Wealth & Relationships

"YOU CAN MAKE MORE FRIENDS IN TWO MONTHS BY BECOMING INTERESTED IN OTHER PEOPLE THAN YOU CAN IN TWO YEARS BY TRYING TO GET OTHER PEOPLE INTERESTED IN YOU." - DALE CARNEGIE

Money and Personal Relationships

Navigating the choppy waters of personal finance within relationships can often feel like an art form. It's a delicate balance between maintaining harmony at home and ensuring both parties are on the same page financially. Let's break it down into manageable parts, starting with how you can talk about finances openly, moving onto managing joint finances effectively, and finally discussing the effects of wealth on your personal relationships.

Discussing Finances in Relationships

Talking about money is often seen as taboo, but in a relationship, it's essential. Start by setting a specific time to discuss finances. This isn't a conversation to have spontaneously in the middle of a supermarket or right after a stressful day at work. Choose a moment when both of you are relaxed and ready to focus on the discussion without distractions.

Begin with your financial goals. What do you both want to achieve in the short term and the long term? These could range from clearing debt, saving for a holiday, investing in property, or planning for retirement. It's crucial that these goals are shared, or at least understood and respected by both parties. This alignment reduces the friction that differing financial priorities can cause.

Transparency is key. Be honest about your current financial situation. This includes disclosing incomes, debts, savings, investments, and even spending habits. It might feel uncomfortable at first, but this openness is the foundation of trust in any relationship.

Remember, this isn't a one-off discussion. Regular check-ins are vital. Markets fluctuate, job situations change, and personal desires evolve. These check-ins keep your financial plans alive, adaptable, and relevant.

Managing Joint Finances

Once you're talking openly about money, the next logical step is to manage it effectively together. There are several ways to do this, and it's all about finding what works best for your partnership.

One common approach is the 'yours, mine, and ours' strategy. Each person maintains their personal account but contributes to a joint account for shared expenses like mortgage payments, utilities, groceries, or holidays. The key here is to agree on how much each person contributes. It could be a 50/50 split, proportional to income, or another arrangement that feels fair to both parties.

Budgeting as a team is also crucial. A joint budget helps you forecast and track your collective financial health. It includes regular expenses, unexpected costs, and savings contributions. Tools like budgeting apps or spreadsheets can simplify this process, providing clarity and preventing disputes.

Always plan for the unexpected. Life throws curveballs, and having a financial buffer can help. This might mean setting aside money in an emergency fund or deciding in advance how to handle sudden large expenses.

Effects of Wealth on Personal Relationships

Wealth can be a blessing or a curse. On the upside, financial security can provide a sense of safety, reduce stress, and offer opportunities that might not otherwise be available. However, it can also introduce complexities into relationships.

One challenge is the change in dynamics that wealth can bring. If there's a significant difference in income or assets between partners, it might lead to feelings of inequality or dependency. Communication and mutual respect are essential in navigating these differences. Acknowledging contributions that aren't financial, such as emotional support, home management, or caregiving, is key.

Another aspect to consider is how wealth impacts social connections. Increased wealth can lead to changes in lifestyle and potentially, in social circles. This can put strain on a relationship if one person feels more comfortable than the other in these new environments or if old friends start to drift away.

Lastly, wealth can lead to complacency. When financial worries are taken off the table, it's easy to neglect the emotional and practical aspects of a relationship that were once driven by necessity. It's important to keep investing in your relationship just as you would with your finances.

Navigating wealth in relationships is about more than just managing money. It's about managing expectations, dreams, and fears. It involves building trust and choosing transparency over convenience. Each step towards financial clarity can also be a step towards a stronger, more resilient relationship.

So, as you tread this path, remember that the goal isn't just to grow your wealth, but also to enrich your relationship. After all, the true value of your bank account isn't just in the figures that represent your balance, but in the joy and security it can bring to you and your loved ones.

Networking for Success

Importance of Building a Network

Imagine this: you're at a bustling industry event, clutching a drink, and you feel slightly out of your depth. Around you are potential contacts, each carrying with them opportunities that could pivot the direction of your career or business. It's not just about collecting business cards but about forging relationships that could open doors to new horizons.

Building a robust network is akin to constructing a safety net for your career or business. The more connections you have, the wider and stronger your safety net becomes. These relationships are valuable assets, often more so than your tangible financial investments because they can provide opportunities, advice, support, and information that are not readily available through other means.

In the pursuit of financial freedom, your network can be your most powerful tool. It's about whom you know, as well as what you know. A diverse network can offer insights into different industries, introduce you to potential mentors, partners, or even lead you to your next big break. Moreover, in an era where industries are continually disrupted by technology and innovation, having a network that spans various sectors and skill sets can help you stay adaptable and relevant.

How to Network Effectively

Networking doesn't come naturally to everyone, but it's a skill that can be honed with practice and strategy. The key is to approach networking not as a means to an immediate end, but as an ongoing process of building relationships.

Firstly, be genuine in your interactions. People are adept at sensing when someone is only speaking to them because they want something. Instead, approach each conversation with curiosity. Learn about the person you're talking to, not just their job title but their interests, challenges, and passions. This approach not only makes the interaction more enjoyable and less pressured for both parties but also forms a connection that is more likely to be remembered.

Secondly, offer value. This doesn't mean you need to offer job leads or introductions right off the bat. Value can be as simple as a thoughtful insight, a book recommendation, or even a listening ear. When you focus on what you can give, rather than what you can get, you build a foundation of reciprocity, which is the bedrock of any strong relationship.

Thirdly, follow up. After meeting someone, send a brief message referencing something you discussed, suggesting a coffee meeting, or simply saying it was nice to meet them. This not only keeps the connection alive but also shows that you value the relationship.

Lastly, leverage social media. Platforms like LinkedIn are invaluable for keeping your network informed about your progress and achievements. Regular updates, when done tastefully, keep you on the radar of your connections and can often lead to unexpected opportunities.

Leveraging Relationships for Financial Opportunities

Once you've built your network, the next step is to leverage these relationships strategically to advance your financial goals. This doesn't mean exploiting your contacts but rather exploring mutually beneficial opportunities.

Start by identifying your goals and then look at how your network can play a role. Are you looking for investors for your startup? Do you need advice on breaking into a particular market? Or perhaps you're seeking a partner for a new venture? Your network is a treasure trove of potential leads and resources.

When tapping into your network, clarity and respect are crucial.

Be clear about what you're asking for. Provide context and be as specific as possible. This helps the other person understand your needs and how they can assist you effectively. Additionally, acknowledge that you are asking for a favour. Respect their time and expertise, and be open to hearing 'no'. Not every interaction will lead to an opportunity, but every interaction well handled strengthens your network.

Another powerful strategy is to look for ways to connect people within your network to each other before you ask for anything in return. Facilitating valuable introductions that benefit others not only enhances your reputation as a connector but also encourages your network to reciprocate when you need assistance.

In the landscape of wealth building, your network can serve as a dynamic ecosystem that supports your growth and opens up new avenues for success. By cultivating strong relationships and engaging with your network thoughtfully, you position yourself to take full advantage of the financial opportunities that come your way. Remember, the strength of your network often determines the height of your success; invest in it wisely.

Mentorship and Coaching

Finding a financial mentor is akin to unlocking a treasure chest of wisdom. It's about discovering that seasoned guide who can navigate you through the tumultuous seas of financial decision-making. Think of a mentor as someone who's travelled the path you're only starting to tread. They've been there, faced those towering waves, and have charted a course to success that you can follow.

So, how do you find this mentor? It starts with clarity. You need to have a clear understanding of your financial goals and the areas where you require guidance. This could range from investment strategies to debt management or even retirement planning. Once you have this mapped out, start looking within your existing networks. Perhaps there's a senior colleague at work, a family friend, or even a professional mentorship program offered through industry associations. If these avenues don't pan out, widen your search. Attend industry seminars, join finance-related workshops, and connect with thought leaders on platforms like LinkedIn. When you do find potential mentors, approach them with specific questions and a genuine interest in their career path and insights. Remember, the relationship should be mutually beneficial; respect their time and show how you can also add value to their professional life.

The benefits of professional coaching can't be overstressed, particularly when you're aiming for financial freedom. A coach offers a more structured and often more intensive relationship than a mentor. While a mentor may help you navigate through advice based on their personal experiences, a coach is there to push your boundaries, set accountability measures, and provide tailored advice to meet your specific challenges. Think of them as your personal financial trainer. They assess your current financial health, identify your strengths and weaknesses, and set up a regimen that helps you achieve optimal results.

Professional coaching can take various forms, from one-on-one sessions to group settings or even online courses. The key is to choose a coach whose expertise aligns with your financial goals and whose approach fits your learning style. An effective coach not only offers guidance but challenges your assumptions, forces you to confront your financial habits, and helps you grow your wealth mindset. Investing in professional coaching might seem like an expense at first, but when you consider the long-term gains – smarter financial decisions, increased wealth, and avoided pitfalls – it's an investment worth making.

Finally, let's talk about how mentorship accelerates success. It's simple: mentors provide shortcuts. Not the kind that cut corners, but the kind that smartly bypass unnecessary mistakes. A good mentor imparts lessons learned from their own experiences, saving you the time and energy you might have spent learning these lessons the hard way. They can open doors to new opportunities and introduce you to key contacts in your industry – think of it as having an all-access pass to professional networks and insider knowledge.

Moreover, mentors can offer you a broader perspective on your career and financial goals, helping you see possibilities you might not have considered. They can challenge you to think bigger and push you towards achieving more than you might on your own. The confidence boost that comes from having a respected figure believing in your capabilities can be a game changer.

In essence, the journey to financial freedom is not just about managing money efficiently; it's equally about choosing who you journey with. Integrating the insights from a mentor and the structured guidance of a coach can elevate your financial game to new heights. Remember, in the quest for wealth, knowledge is currency, and by leveraging mentorship and coaching, you're essentially investing in the best kind of wealth accumulation there is – intellectual capital.

So, as you forge ahead in your pursuit of financial freedom, consider how both mentorship and professional coaching could fit into your strategy. These relationships could very well be the catalysts that propel you towards your financial goals faster and more effectively than you ever imagined possible.

Summary & Application Exercises

Navigating the complex interplay between wealth and relationships is crucial for anyone aiming for financial freedom. Understanding how money interweaves with personal relationships, networking, and mentorship can significantly alter your approach to building and maintaining wealth.

Firstly, addressing finances within personal relationships is not just important; it's imperative. Make it a habit to discuss financial goals and budgets openly with your partner. This transparency fosters trust and prevents conflicts. Here's your action step: schedule a monthly financial date night where you review your financial plans and progress together.

Secondly, managing joint finances efficiently can safeguard

your financial future and strengthen your relationship. Create a joint account for shared expenses but also maintain individual accounts for personal spending. Action step? Set up these accounts if you haven't already, and start a shared spreadsheet to track your contributions and expenditures.

Thirdly, wealth can influence personal dynamics, often intensifying emotions and stakes. Always strive to keep communication lines open, and consider consulting a financial advisor or therapist if money becomes a contentious issue. Your action step here is to list down any signs of stress or strain in relationships due to financial issues and address them proactively.

Moving on to networking, remember that your network can significantly impact your financial and professional growth. Make a plan to attend at least one networking event or seminar each quarter where you can meet potential mentors, partners, or investors. Your immediate action step is to research events in your industry and put them in your calendar.

Effective networking means being genuine and helpful. Always think about how you can add value to your connections before considering what you can gain. Start by reconnecting with old colleagues or peers via email or social media and offer something of value—information, introductions, or support.

Leveraging relationships for financial opportunities requires tact and integrity. Ensure you're seen as trustworthy and reliable. As an action step, identify at least three people in your network who could be key to unlocking new opportunities and plan how you can strengthen these relationships.

Lastly, in the realm of mentorship and coaching, finding a financial mentor can be a game-changer. Identify someone whose financial path you admire and reach out for guidance. Remember, mentorship is a two-way street; consider what you can bring to the table as well.

The benefits of professional coaching are manifold. Investing in coaching could accelerate your success, providing you with tailored advice and accountability. Why not research potential coaches this week?

Mentorship accelerates success not just by providing guidance but also by expanding your perspective. If you haven't found a mentor yet, make it your goal to attend events or join forums where potential mentors might be present.

By integrating these practices into your life, you'll not only enhance your financial profile but also enrich your personal and professional relationships. Start implementing these steps today, and watch how they open new avenues to achieving financial freedom.

Notes & Reflections

The Science of Spending

"Too many people spend money they haven't earned, to buy things they don't want, to impress people they don't like." - Will Rogers

Smart Spending Habits

In the quest for financial freedom, how you manage your spending can either be your greatest ally or your most formidable foe. It's not just about how much money you can make, but also about how wisely you can spend it. Let's dive into the art of smart spending, which is less about scrimping and saving every penny, and more about spending with intention and insight.

Conscious Consumption

Conscious consumption starts with understanding the difference between wants and needs. This might sound straightforward, but in a world filled with marketing gimmicks and impulse-buy triggers, it can be anything but. Every pound spent should be seen as an investment in your life. Before you part with your cash, ask yourself: Is this purchase going to enhance my life? Will it bring lasting happiness, utility, or improvement to my daily existence?

Consider the concept of 'cost per use', a simple yet powerful way to evaluate purchases. For instance, buying a quality pair of shoes for £100 that you'll wear every day for a year offers a better cost per use than a trendy £50 pair that wears out after a few outings. This approach not only makes you think twice about the quality and longevity of what you buy but also steers you away from the throwaway culture that's detrimental to both your wallet and the planet.

Furthermore, conscious consumption means staying informed about the products you buy and the companies you support. In today's digital age, it's easier than ever to research the ethics, sustainability, and corporate practices behind brands. Choosing to support businesses that align with your values can contribute to a broader sense of well-being and satisfaction.

Budgeting for Happiness

Yes, budgeting can indeed be aligned with happiness. It's all about ensuring that your spending reflects your values and what truly brings joy into your life. This starts with setting up a budget that categorises expenses not just by necessity, but by the joy they bring. Allocate funds for experiences or items that have proven to yield happiness and personal growth, such as travel, books, or fitness classes.

The key here is to remember that budgeting isn't about restriction; it's about making room for what enriches your life. For example, if dining out with friends every Friday night is something that you cherish, make sure your budget accommodates that by perhaps cutting back on other less rewarding expenses like unused subscriptions or habitual impulse buys.

Additionally, a part of budgeting for happiness is preparing for the unexpected. An emergency fund isn't just a financial buffer but also a peace of mind fund. Knowing you have a financial cushion can reduce stress and allow you to enjoy your daily life without the constant worry of potential financial disasters.

Avoiding Impulsive Spending

Impulsive spending is often the arch-nemesis of financial freedom. It's the quick, emotional decision that bypasses rational thought and long-term planning. Combatting this doesn't just start with self-control; it involves creating systems that help foster more mindful spending.

One effective strategy is the 24-hour rule. When faced with a non-essential purchase, give yourself 24 hours to think about it. This cooling-off period can help you determine if the item is something you truly need or just a fleeting desire. Often, you'll find that the urge to buy dissipates after some reflection.

Another useful approach is to use cash or a debit card for daily transactions instead of a credit card. The physical act of handing over cash makes the spending feel more real than just swiping a card, which can sometimes feel like playing with Monopoly money. This can slow you down and make you think twice about each purchase.

Lastly, keep track of your spending. Whether it's through a smartphone app or a simple spreadsheet, regularly seeing where your money goes can be an eye-opener. You might discover patterns of impulsive buying that you weren't even aware of. Knowledge is power, and knowing your spending habits gives you the power to change them.

By adopting these smart spending habits, you're not just saving money; you're also building a foundation for a financially secure and fulfilling life. It's about making every pound work not just for you, but for the life you want to lead. Remember, financial freedom isn't just about accumulating wealth, but about making informed, conscious decisions that pave the way to a prosperous and happy existence.

Investing in Yourself

Education and Personal Development

In the journey to financial freedom, one of the smartest investments you can ever make is in your own education and personal development. Think of it this way: every skill you acquire doubles your odds of success. It's not just about formal education; it's about continuously enhancing your knowledge and skills to stay relevant and competitive in today's fast-paced world.

Start by identifying the skills that are in high demand within your industry and beyond. Technology and business landscapes are evolving rapidly, and skills like digital literacy, leadership, and critical thinking are becoming indispensable. Online courses, workshops, and seminars can be invaluable, and many are offered for free or at a minimal cost. Platforms like Coursera, Udemy, and LinkedIn Learning are treasure troves of knowledge, covering everything from blockchain technology to creative writing.

But it's not all about hard skills. Soft skills, such as communication, emotional intelligence, and adaptability, are equally crucial. They enable you to navigate the workplace more effectively and forge better relationships. Remember, investing in your personal development also involves nurturing your creativity and innovation — key drivers that can propel you to the top of your professional game.

Health as an Investment

It's easy to overlook health when talking about financial planning, but let's get one thing straight: your health is an investment, not an expense. Without good health, achieving any kind of success, financial or otherwise, can become a distant dream. Think of maintaining your health as you would a high-performance engine; regular upkeep is essential.

Nutrition plays a foundational role. Investing in a diet rich in fruits, vegetables, lean proteins, and whole grains can boost your productivity and energy levels. It's not about short-term diets but sustainable eating habits that will fuel your body and mind for the long haul. And while you might think skipping on health foods or gym memberships will save money, consider the long-term costs of medical bills from chronic diseases that could have been preventable.

Physical activity is equally important. Regular exercise not only improves physical health but also mental health by reducing anxiety, depression, and negative mood by improving self-esteem and cognitive function. You don't necessarily need an expensive gym membership. Walking, cycling, home workouts, or even active hobbies like gardening can keep you fit without breaking the bank.

Finally, never underestimate the value of sleep. Adequate sleep is crucial for recovery, memory retention, and overall well-being. It's the ultimate form of rest and recovery for both your body and mind.

The Importance of Work-Life Balance

Achieving work-life balance is not just a trendy buzzword; it's a critical component of long-term success and personal satisfaction. The grind culture might glorify working 24/7, but in the long run, this is unsustainable and can lead to burnout. What's the point of achieving financial freedom if you're too stressed or burnt out to enjoy it?

Balancing your professional and personal life allows you to recharge and return to your work more focused and motivated. It also opens up opportunities to pursue hobbies and interests, spend time with loved ones, and relax, which can significantly boost your mental health and overall happiness. Remember, a well-rounded life fosters a sharp mind and a robust spirit capable of tackling challenges and seizing opportunities.

To achieve this balance, start by setting boundaries. Learn to say no when work demands encroach on your personal time. Make use of technology smartly — let it help you manage your tasks more efficiently rather than be a source of endless distraction. Prioritise your tasks based on importance and urgency, and be realistic about what you can achieve within a given timeframe.

Also, make time for yourself. It might seem counterintuitive when there are deadlines looming, but taking short breaks during long tasks helps maintain a high level of performance. During these breaks, avoid thinking about work. Engage in quick stretches, a brief walk, or a relaxation technique. This not only helps reduce stress but also boosts your productivity when you get back to work.

Investing in yourself by enhancing your education and skills, maintaining your health, and achieving work-life balance are crucial steps towards not just financial success but also personal fulfilment. Each of these elements supports the other, creating a robust foundation for achieving and enjoying your financial goals. Remember, the best investment you can make is in yourself — after all, you're the most important asset you'll ever have.

Financial Contributions and Charity

The Role of Philanthropy in Wealth

You might think that philanthropy is only for the ultra-rich, the kind of people who have buildings and endowments named after them. But here's a little secret: engaging in philanthropy, regardless of the scale, can be a pivotal part of building and maintaining wealth, not just for you but for generations to come.

Philanthropy helps you establish a network of influence and respect. It's not just about giving money away; it's about creating connections with other individuals who are capable of making large-scale changes in the world. These connections can lead to partnerships, business opportunities, and even more effective ways to multiply your impact and assets.

Moreover, engaging in charitable activities can enhance your reputation. In a world where businesses and individuals are increasingly judged by their contribution to society, being seen as a proactive giver can differentiate you from competitors, potentially attracting more clients or customers who value social responsibility.

Another compelling reason to integrate philanthropy into your wealth-building strategy is the psychological and emotional returns. Studies have shown that giving to others can significantly boost your mood and overall mental health, which can improve your decision-making abilities and outlook on life—including the way you manage your business and personal finances.

Choosing Charities and Causes

Choosing where to invest your charitable dollars is as crucial as selecting stocks or real estate investments. It requires thought, research, and a keen understanding of what you hope to achieve through your financial contributions. Start by identifying causes that resonate with you personally. Are you passionate about education, or perhaps healthcare? Maybe environmental conservation pulls on your heartstrings? Selecting a cause that you feel emotionally connected to can enhance the satisfaction and fulfillment derived from giving.

Once you've pinpointed your interests, it's time to do some homework. Look into charities that not only support your chosen cause but also have a robust track record of success and transparency. Resources like Charity Navigator or the UK's Charity Commission provide detailed analyses of how charities utilise contributions, helping you ensure that your money is actually going towards the cause rather than getting swallowed up in administrative costs.

Consider also the scalability and impact of your contributions. Sometimes, smaller, local charities have a more direct impact on their communities and might offer more meaningful opportunities for personal involvement. On the other hand, larger organisations might provide broader, more systemic change within their fields.

The Impact of Giving Back on Personal Wealth

Intuitively, it might seem that giving your money away would diminish your wealth. However, when done strategically, philanthropy can actually enhance your financial status. There's a reason why many wealthy individuals and successful businesses make a point of publicly announcing their charitable donations. Beyond the tax benefits—which are, admittedly, quite appealing—giving back can lead to increased wealth through several less direct, but equally powerful, avenues.

Firstly, philanthropy can serve as a form of legacy building, helping to cement your personal or business brand in the collective memory as something positive and benevolent. This kind of reputation management is invaluable and can often lead to increased business opportunities. People like to do business with those they perceive as ethical and generous.

Moreover, giving back to the community can lead to personal growth. Engaging with different communities and issues can provide new perspectives that improve your empathy and emotional intelligence. These traits are incredibly beneficial in business and personal relationships, potentially leading to more profound and more productive connections.

Lastly, let's not overlook the networking aspect. Charity events and philanthropic boards are often teeming with successful, like-minded individuals. Participating in these circles can provide you with unique networking opportunities that might not arise in other business contexts. Here, connections are made on a foundation of shared values and respect, which can often lead to more substantial and enduring professional relationships.

So, while the cheque you write today might decrease your bank balance slightly, the long-term benefits of philanthropy could multiply your wealth in ways that are not immediately financial but are profoundly impactful. Whether it's through enhanced reputation, personal growth, or networking opportunities, integrating charity into your financial planning is more than a noble endeavour—it's a smart one.

Summary & Application Exercises

Congratulations on completing this crucial chapter on mastering the art of spending wisely. By now, you've dived deep into smart spending habits, investing in yourself, and understanding the significance of financial contributions and charity. Let's ensure that these concepts don't just remain ideas, but transform into actionable steps that pave your way to financial freedom.

1. **Conscious Consumption**: Start by reviewing your current spending. Keep a daily log for one month to identify where your money actually goes. This will help you spot unnecessary expenses or habits that you can cut back on. Remember, every penny saved is a penny earned towards your financial freedom.

2. **Budgeting for Happiness:** Allocate funds specifically for activities that bring you joy and satisfaction. Whether it's a hobby, travel, or spending time with loved ones, ensure your budget reflects these priorities. This approach not only makes life enjoyable but also sustainable, keeping you motivated on your financial journey.

3. **Avoiding Impulsive Spending**: Create a 48-hour rule for all non-essential purchases. If you feel the urge to buy something, note it down and revisit it after 48 hours. Often, you'll find that the impulse fades, saving you from unnecessary expenses.

4. **Education and Personal Development:** Invest in skills and knowledge that enhance your earning potential. Whether it's an online course, books, or workshops, choose resources that align with your career goals and personal interests. Remember, self-improvement is a continuous process.

5. **Health as an Investment:** Never compromise on your health. Regular exercise, a balanced diet, and adequate sleep are non-negotiable for maintaining high energy levels and focus. Consider health expenses as investments, not costs.

6. **Work-Life Balance: Deliberately plan downtime and stick to it as rigorously as your work schedule. Balance helps prevent burnout and keeps you efficient and sharp in your professional and personal life.

7. **The Role of Philanthropy in Wealth:** Identify causes that resonate with your values and consider setting aside a portion of your income or time for these. Philanthropy can enrich your life, give you a sense of purpose, and even connect you with like-minded individuals.

8. **Choosing Charities and Causes**: Do thorough research to ensure that your contributions are used effectively. Look for transparency in operations and clear evidence of impact.

9. **The Impact of Giving Back on Personal Wealth:** Reflect on how giving makes you richer—not just financially but in happiness and satisfaction. Document these feelings as they can be incredibly reinforcing in continuing your journey of generosity.

By integrating these principles into your daily life, you are not just spending money; you're investing in your future. Take these steps seriously, apply them consistently, and watch as you build a life of wealth and satisfaction. Remember, the path to financial freedom isn't just about making money, but making smart choices with your resources.

Notes & Reflections

Mastering the Markets

"The stock market is filled with individuals who know the price of everything, but the value of nothing." - Philip Fisher

Understanding Market Basics

In the bustling world of finance, the stock market is essentially the beating heart. It's where fortunes can be made and dreams can be realised, but only if you know how to navigate its intricate dance. Let's break down the essentials, shall we?

Stock Markets 101

Imagine the stock market as a grand marketplace, not unlike the bustling bazaars of Istanbul or the vibrant streets of Camden Market. Instead of buying carpets or vintage clothes, you're trading shares of companies. These shares represent a small part of ownership in a company. When the company does well, the value of your shares might increase. Conversely, if the company hits a rough patch, the value of your shares could decrease.

The key players in this market are like the diverse characters you might find in any market scene. There are individual investors like you, big institutional investors (think giant funds that manage pensions or endowments), and everyone in between. Each has different goals and strategies, but all are united by the same aim: to make money.

Navigating this market starts with understanding its nature. It operates on supply and demand. When a stock is desired by many but available in small quantities, the price tends to rise. If it's available in abundance but no one really wants it, the price tends to fall. Simple, right?

But here's where it gets exciting. The stock market is influenced by countless factors—from global economic news to market sentiment, even to weather events affecting commodity prices. Your role as an investor is to analyse these factors and make educated guesses about future stock movements.

How Global Economics Affect Investments

Global economics might sound like a complex, far-removed concept, but it's closer to your investment portfolio than you might think. Global economic health influences how markets move, interest rates, and even commodity prices—all of which can affect your investments.

For instance, if a major economy like the USA or China experiences rapid growth, markets worldwide often rally. Companies in these countries might report higher profits, which in turn boosts investor confidence and increases stock prices. Conversely, if there's a recession, fear can grip the market, prices may drop, and investing becomes more like a game of hot potato.

Currency fluctuations also play a crucial part. If you're holding stocks in a currency that weakens against your home currency, the value of your returns might decrease when converted back to your local currency. Hence, keeping an eye on global economic indicators—like GDP growth rates, unemployment rates, and inflation—is crucial.

Reading Market Trends

Understanding market trends is like learning to read the weather before a sailing trip. It helps you navigate your investment journey more smoothly. Trends can be short-term or long-term; they can be based on economic cycles or specific industry growth patterns.

Technical analysis and fundamental analysis are two techniques used to analyse market trends. Technical analysis involves studying charts of past market data to predict future price movements. It's akin to recognising the formation of storm clouds and anticipating rain. Fundamental analysis, on the other hand, delves into a company's financial statements, market position, and economic factors to judge its potential for growth—like assessing the health of a tree by examining its roots.

For instance, if you notice a trend where tech stocks are consistently climbing over several months, this could indicate a longer-term movement towards technology-driven investments. Alternatively, if financial news reports a sudden interest rate increase, you might observe a short-term dip in the stock market as investors adjust to the new conditions.

Both types of analysis can help you make informed decisions. By understanding how to read these market trends, you equip yourself with the knowledge to anticipate market movements rather than just reacting to them.

As you embark on this thrilling journey of stock market investing, remember that knowledge is your most valuable asset. By understanding the basics, keeping an eye on global economics, and learning to read market trends, you're laying a solid foundation for your financial freedom. Dive in, stay curious, and let the market be your teacher.

Advanced Investment Strategies

When you're ready to move beyond the basics of the stock market, it's vital to arm yourself with a set of strategies that can enhance your investment portfolio. The complexities of the financial world might seem daunting, but with the right approaches—such as diversification, understanding risk management, and distinguishing between short-term and long-term investments—you can navigate the markets more effectively and aim towards achieving your financial goals.

Portfolio Diversification

Think of diversification as your financial safety net. It's the process of spreading your investments across various asset classes and sectors to reduce risk. The logic here is straightforward: different assets perform differently under various economic conditions. By diversifying, you're not putting all your eggs in one basket, and thus you buffer your investments against significant losses.

Diversification isn't just about adding different stocks to your portfolio. It extends to other asset classes like bonds, commodities, real estate, and even geographic locations. For instance, international stocks can provide growth opportunities in emerging markets that domestic stocks may not. Furthermore, sectors like technology and healthcare might react differently to the same economic event compared to, say, consumer goods or manufacturing.

To implement this strategy effectively, you'll need to evaluate assets based on how they correlate with each other. The goal is to combine assets that do not move in tandem; this way, when one investment is down, another might be up, balancing the overall performance of your portfolio.

Risk Management Techniques

Risk management is crucial in investing. It's all about identifying, analysing, and taking steps to minimise the uncertainties in your investment decisions. Effective risk management can be the difference between achieving steady growth and suffering unexpected losses.

One fundamental technique is setting stop-loss orders. A stop-loss is an order placed with a broker to sell a security when it reaches a certain price. It's designed to limit an investor's loss on a security position. For example, if you buy a stock at £100 and set a stop-loss order at £90, your loss is capped at10% if the stock's price plummets.

Another technique is the use of options and futures contracts as a form of insurance against price fluctuations. Options give you the right, but not the obligation, to buy or sell an asset at a predetermined price before a certain expiry date. This can help protect against downside risk while allowing you to benefit from upside potential.

Risk tolerance is also a personal aspect that varies from one investor to another. It's influenced by your financial goals, investment horizon, and personal comfort with uncertainty. Regularly assessing your risk tolerance is important as it can change over time with alterations in your financial situation, life events, or even shifts in market conditions.

Long-term vs. Short-term Investing

Understanding the difference between long-term and short-term investing and knowing when to apply each strategy can significantly impact your investment success. Long-term investments are typically held for several years or even decades. These investments can ride out market volatility and benefit from the power of compounding interest. Stocks, mutual funds, and real estate often fall into this category.

In contrast, short-term investments are usually held for less than a year and require a more active management strategy. They can include trading stocks, commodities, or currencies where quick gains from market movements are the goal. However, they also come with higher risk and higher potential costs from transaction fees and taxes.

Deciding between long-term and short-term investing should align with your financial goals, risk tolerance, and time horizon. For retirement savings, a long-term approach is typically recommended. But if you're saving for a near-term goal, like buying a home in the next couple of years, a short-term strategy might be more appropriate.

Each has its merits and risks. Long-term investing tends to be less stressful and less labor-intensive since it doesn't require constant market monitoring. It also benefits from the tendency of markets to rise over extended periods. Short-term investing, on the other hand, can generate quick returns but requires more expertise and a greater appetite for risk. It's also more sensitive to market timing, and getting this wrong can be costly.

By understanding and implementing these advanced investment strategies—diversification, risk management, and distinguishing between long-term and short-term investing—you enhance your ability to navigate through the complexities of the financial markets. This not only helps in protecting your investment capital but also sets a solid foundation for potential growth, moving you closer to financial freedom. Remember, the key is not just to invest but to invest wisely.

Innovations in Investing

Investing has always been a dynamic field, evolving with each technological advancement and macroeconomic shift. Today, the landscape is almost unrecognisable compared to just a decade ago, thanks to significant innovations that are shaping the way you invest and manage your finances. Let's dive into how technology is revolutionising investing, the role of cryptocurrencies and blockchain, and take a glimpse into what the future might hold for financial markets.

Impact of Technology on Investing

The digital age has ushered in a new era where technology is at the forefront of investment strategies. One of the most significant advancements has been the rise of algorithmic trading. These are computer programs that use complex algorithms to analyse multiple markets and execute trades at speeds and volumes that are unattainable by human traders. This technology enables you to maximise efficiencies and potentially increase returns while minimising risk.

Beyond trading, technology has also democratised access to the markets through platforms that offer low-cost, sometimes even free, trading options. Apps and platforms like Robinhood or eToro have broken down barriers that once made investing accessible only to the financially affluent or those with a deep understanding of financial markets. Now, with a smartphone and internet connection, virtually everyone has the ability to start building their investment portfolio.

Furthermore, artificial intelligence (AI) and machine learning are now being employed to predict market trends and make more informed investment decisions. These systems analyse vast amounts of data — from market indicators to social media sentiment — to identify potential investment opportunities or risks. For you, this means a tool that complements your market insights with data-driven analysis, enhancing your ability to make strategic investment decisions.

Cryptocurrency and Blockchain

Perhaps no other innovation has sparked as much debate and excitement as cryptocurrency and blockchain technology. Bitcoin, the first cryptocurrency, introduced a new form of digital currency in 2009 that operates independently of a central authority. The underlying technology, blockchain, ensures security and transparency through a decentralized ledger system where transactions are recorded and confirmed anonymously.

Investing in cryptocurrencies can be highly volatile, but it also offers high reward potential. For instance, early investors in Bitcoin saw astronomical returns as its value skyrocketed from a few cents to thousands of pounds. However, this market remains speculative and is influenced by factors ranging from technological developments to regulatory changes and market sentiment.

Blockchain technology, on the other hand, has implications far beyond cryptocurrencies. It is being explored for its potential to revolutionise various sectors, including finance, by streamlining operations and reducing costs. Smart contracts, which automatically execute transactions when certain conditions are met, are just one example of how blockchain can be utilised to enhance the efficiency and security of financial transactions.

For you, understanding cryptocurrency and blockchain is crucial, not only to diversify your investment portfolio but also to stay ahead in a world where these technologies may soon become as standard as stocks and bonds.

The Future of Financial Markets

Looking ahead, the future of financial markets appears ripe with potential, driven largely by ongoing innovations. One area to watch is the integration of Internet of Things (IoT) technology with investing. IoT devices can provide real-time data that could impact markets instantly. For example, sensors that track agricultural conditions could inform commodity trading decisions, providing you with an edge in market predictions.

Moreover, the rise of green finance and impact investing reflects a growing trend of investors not just seeking financial returns, but also wanting to make a positive impact on the world. Financial markets are responding with more opportunities to invest in sustainable and socially responsible ways. This shift not only helps address global challenges but also opens up new investment avenues for you to explore, aligning financial goals with personal values.

Additionally, the increasing sophistication of financial technology (fintech) startups is likely to continue disrupting traditional banking and investment services. These companies often focus on specific niche problems, offering solutions that are more efficient, less costly, and more user-friendly than those provided by traditional financial institutions. For you, this means more choices, better services, and potentially higher returns.

The landscape of investing is continually changing, influenced by technological advancements, evolving market conditions, and new financial instruments. Staying informed and adaptable will be key to your success in navigating this dynamic environment. As you look toward building wealth and achieving financial freedom, embrace these innovations with an open mind and a strategic approach, ensuring that you not only keep pace with the evolving market but also capitalise on opportunities that these innovations bring.

Summary & Application Exercises

Congratulations! You've just navigated through the complexities of Mastering the Markets. You now understand the foundational elements of stock markets, the influence of global economics on investments, and how to read market trends. You've also explored advanced investment strategies including diversifying your portfolio, managing risks, and choosing between long-term and short-term investments. Finally, you delved into the innovative world of technology in investing, cryptocurrency, blockchain, and pondered the future of financial markets.

Armed with this knowledge, you're better equipped to make informed decisions that align with your financial goals. Here are some actionable steps to take your investment journey to the next level:

1. **Educate Yourself Continuously**: The market is dynamic,

and staying informed is key. Subscribe to financial news outlets, follow market trends, and keep learning. Resources like podcasts, webinars, and books can be invaluable.

2. **Evaluate Your Financial Goals**: Sit down and clearly define what you want to achieve. Are you saving for retirement, a home, or perhaps your children's education? Your investment decisions should align with these goals.

3. **Start Small**: If you're new to investing, start with small, manageable amounts of money. Use online investment platforms to make the process easier and more accessible.

4. **Diversify Your Portfolio**: Don't put all your eggs in one basket. Spread your investments across different assets to mitigate risk. Include a mix of stocks, bonds, and perhaps some cryptocurrency if you're comfortable with its volatility.

5. **Develop a Risk Management Strategy**: Decide in advance how much risk you are willing to take on and set up mechanisms to mitigate losses, such as stop-loss orders.

6. **Consider Long-Term Investments**: Building wealth is a marathon, not a sprint. Consider long-term investments that compound over time, and be patient.

7. **Stay Updated on Technological Advances**: Technology is reshaping investing. Keep an eye on new tools and platforms that can enhance your investing process.

8. **Experiment with Simulations**: Before committing real

money, try using investment simulations. Many platforms offer simulated trading environments where you can practice without financial risk.

9. **Join Investment Communities**: Engage with other investors through forums, clubs, or social media groups. These communities can provide support, insights, and networking opportunities.

10. **Review and Adjust Regularly**: Check your investment portfolio periodically and make adjustments as needed. Market conditions change, and so should your strategy.

By taking these steps, you'll not only become more confident in your investment choices but also move closer to achieving financial freedom. Remember, the journey to mastering the markets is ongoing—the more proactive and prepared you are, the better your chances of success. Happy investing!

Notes & Reflections

Legacy & Wealth Preservation

"The greatness of a man is measured by the way he treats the little man. Compassion for the weak is a sign of greatness." - Myles Munroe

Planning for the Future

When you think about your future, what visions do you have? Maybe it's the peace of knowing your family will be secure after you're gone, or perhaps it's the idea of your legacy living on through generations. But to turn these visions into reality, you need a robust plan. Let's delve into the essentials of future planning: estate planning, creating a will, and utilising trusts and other legal tools. These aren't just tasks for the wealthy; they're crucial steps for anyone who wishes to manage their financial future effectively.

Estate Planning

Estate planning sounds like something out of an old British drama—something only aristocrats worry about. But it's actually a critical process for anyone wanting to manage their assets responsibly. It's about organising your assets to ensure they are distributed according to your wishes upon your death, minimising legal hurdles and taxes.

The first step in estate planning is to take stock of what you own—properties, investments, savings, and personal possessions. Knowing what's in your estate is crucial to managing it. Next, think about your family's needs. Who depends on you financially? How can you ensure their financial security after you're gone?

It's also wise to consider the tax implications of your estate. In the UK, for instance, estates valued over a certain threshold may be subject to Inheritance Tax. However, with careful planning, such as gifting assets during your lifetime, you can significantly reduce this burden.

Consulting with a financial advisor or an estate planner can help you navigate these waters. They can offer tailored advice based on your specific circumstances, ensuring that your estate is as tax-efficient as possible. Remember, estate planning is not a 'set and forget' task. It should evolve as your life does, from changes in your family to fluctuations in your assets.

Creating a Will

If estate planning is the blueprint, a will is the foundation. Creating a will is fundamental to ensuring your assets are distributed as you wish. Without a will, you're leaving the distribution of your assets up to the laws of intestacy, which might not reflect your personal wishes and could lead to family disputes.

Writing a will can seem daunting, but it doesn't have to be. Start by listing who you want to inherit your assets, known as your beneficiaries. These can be family members, friends, or even charities. Next, decide who will execute your will, known as the executor. This person will manage the distribution of your estate, so choose someone who is trustworthy and capable.

For parents, a will is also the place to appoint guardians for your children in case both parents pass away. This is arguably one of the most critical decisions you can make, so it's important to discuss it thoroughly with the chosen guardians to ensure they are willing and able to take on the responsibility.

While DIY will-writing kits are available, investing in legal advice can prevent mistakes that could make your will invalid. A solicitor can ensure that your will complies with legal standards and truly reflects your wishes.

Trusts and Other Legal Tools

Trusts are another powerful tool in your estate planning arsenal. They allow you to set aside assets for specific purposes, such as funding your children's education or donating to charity. Trusts can also help reduce your Inheritance Tax liability and can offer protection against creditors.

Setting up a trust can be complex, and the right type of trust depends on your individual circumstances. For instance, a discretionary trust gives the trustees (the people you appoint to manage the trust) the power to decide how the assets are used. This is particularly useful if your beneficiaries are young children or if you want to preserve flexibility for future circumstances.

Other legal tools include Lasting Powers of Attorney (LPA). An LPA allows you to appoint someone to make decisions on your behalf if you become unable to do so yourself. There are two types of LPA: one for financial decisions and one for health and care decisions. Setting up an LPA ensures that someone you trust is making decisions in your best interest, should you become incapacitated.

Future planning isn't just about securing your own peace of mind; it's about providing for and protecting those you care about. By taking control of your estate planning, drafting a will, and understanding the role of trusts and other legal tools, you're not just planning for the future—you're shaping it. Remember, the best time to plan for tomorrow is today.

Protecting Your Assets

When it comes to safeguarding the wealth you've worked so hard to accumulate, understanding your insurance options, the legal protections available, and the means to secure your digital assets becomes not just important, but essential. Let's dive into these crucial elements to ensure that your financial fortress stands robust against the various threats that could undermine its stability.

Insurance Options

Insurance isn't the sexiest topic under the sun, but think of it as a superhero cape for your assets—it's there to protect you when disaster strikes. Navigating the world of insurance policies might feel like trying to read a map in a foreign language, but it's crucial for preserving your hard-earned wealth. So, where do you start?

Firstly, consider what you need to protect. Property and casualty insurance are the basics, covering your home and possessions from damage or theft. But beyond that, there are several other types of insurance that might be relevant depending on your circumstances. For instance, liability insurance is an absolute must if you're in a profession or run a business where there's a risk of being sued. This type of insurance can help cover legal fees and any potential settlements, keeping your assets safe from legal disputes.

Then there's life insurance, a cornerstone in protecting your family's future financial stability. Deciding between term and whole life insurance policies will depend on your financial goals and needs. Term insurance, generally less expensive, covers you for a set period—useful for covering needs that aren't permanent, like an outstanding mortgage or education for your kids. Whole life insurance, on the other hand, not only provides a death benefit but also includes an investment component that can grow tax-deferred. This can be a part of your wealth-building strategy, accumulating cash value that you can borrow against if needed.

Critical illness and disability insurance are also important, safeguarding your income should you become seriously ill or disabled and unable to work. These policies help ensure that even if your physical condition forces you out of work, your financial health remains robust.

Legal Protections for Wealth

Having legal barriers in place to protect your wealth is like building a moat around your castle. The first line of defence is often setting up the right kind of ownership structure for your assets. For example, holding property jointly with a spouse or partner can offer a layer of protection against creditors in some jurisdictions. Alternatively, if you're a business owner, incorporating your business can help shield your personal assets from business liabilities.

Another powerful tool in your legal armoury could be a limited liability company (LLC) or a family limited partnership (FLP). These structures can offer substantial protection for your assets, while also providing flexibility in how those assets are managed and controlled. They can limit your liability to the amount you've invested in the LLC or FLP, protecting your other assets from being at risk.

But legal protection isn't just about shielding assets—it's also about ensuring that your wishes are respected. This is where powers of attorney (POA) and living wills come into play. A POA allows you to appoint someone to manage your affairs if you're unable to do so, ensuring that someone you trust is at the helm. A living will specifies your wishes regarding medical treatment if you become incapacitated, protecting your personal wishes even when you can't voice them.

Safeguarding Digital Assets

In today's digital age, your online presence and digital assets are an integral part of your wealth. These can include everything from digital wallets and cryptocurrencies to online businesses and social media accounts. Safeguarding these requires a mix of technical know-how and strategic planning.

First, think security—strong, unique passwords for each account, enabled two-factor authentication, and the use of secure, encrypted connections can help protect your digital valuables from cyber threats. Consider using a password manager to keep track of your passwords while maintaining high security.

Next, consider the legal aspects of your digital assets. Ensure that your digital assets are included in your estate planning. Many online platforms now allow you to designate a legacy contact or set up directives about what should happen to your accounts in the event of your death. For digital currencies like Bitcoin, ensure that your digital wallets and their keys are safely stored and that instructions for accessing them are included in your estate plans, possibly within a digital will.

Lastly, keep a digital inventory. This includes a list of all your online accounts, digital assets, and important digital files, along with instructions on how they should be managed. This not only helps in managing them during your lifetime but also ensures they are taken care of according to your wishes after you're gone.

In conclusion, protecting your assets is an ongoing process that requires you to stay informed and proactive. Whether it's through choosing the right insurance policies, setting up legal structures to shield your wealth, or securing your digital life, taking these steps will help ensure that the wealth you've accumulated continues to serve you and your loved ones well into the future.

Passing on Wealth

Strategies for Inheritance

When it comes to passing on your accumulated wealth, the what and the how can truly shape the legacy you leave behind. It's not just about ensuring that your heirs receive something in your will, but about the impact and utility of what they receive. Think of it as strategic generosity.

One approach is the outright bequest, where assets are transferred directly to your heirs upon your death. This is straightforward but doesn't allow for much control over how the wealth is used. To navigate this, consider staggered inheritances. This can involve releasing funds at certain ages or milestones, like graduating from university or buying a first home. It's a method that can instil responsibility and prevent financial missteps.

Another effective strategy is the use of specific bequests for particular purposes, like education or charitable giving. This can help inculcate values you deem important and ensure that your wealth fosters positive outcomes. For example, setting up a scholarship fund in your name not only aids your descendants but also extends your influence into the lives of others, creating a ripple effect of your values.

For those with substantial assets, creating a family limited partnership can be a savvy manoeuvre. It allows you to transfer business interests to your heirs while retaining control during your lifetime. Plus, it can offer tax benefits, which is always a bonus.

Lastly, remember that tax implications are a crucial part of any inheritance strategy. Consulting with a tax advisor to navigate inheritance tax and potential loopholes could save your heirs a significant amount in the long run. After all, it's not just about what you leave, but what's left after taxes.

Educating the Next Generation on Wealth Management

Now, let's talk about arguably the most critical aspect of wealth transmission: education. Handing over wealth without the necessary wisdom to manage it is like handing over the keys of a sports car to a novice driver. Exciting, but potentially disastrous.

Start early by integrating discussions about money into everyday life. This doesn't mean overwhelming young children with complex investment strategies but discussing topics like saving or budgeting in age-appropriate ways. As they grow, so should their financial education, evolving into more complex subjects such as investing, real estate, and entrepreneurship.

Consider formalising this education through structured family wealth education programs. These can be as simple as regular meetings to discuss the state of family finances or as elaborate as hiring financial advisors to conduct seminars on different aspects of wealth management.

Also, leverage technology. There are myriad tools and apps designed to teach financial literacy in an engaging way. This can be particularly effective for tech-savvy younger generations who might prefer digital learning platforms over traditional methods.

Remember, the goal is to cultivate a mindset that views wealth not as a means to material end but as a tool for creating value for themselves and others. It's about preparing them to not just sustain, but to enhance the family wealth.

Family Wealth Meetings

Finally, the glue that holds all these efforts together is communication. Regular family wealth meetings are essential. They serve as a forum for discussing financial matters, sharing updates, and making collective decisions about the family's assets. Think of it as a board meeting for your family's future.

These meetings should be structured but not stiff. Set an agenda, keep minutes, and have clear objectives for each meeting. However, ensure there's room for all voices to be heard. This inclusivity reinforces the sense of responsibility among family members and helps foster a collaborative approach to wealth management.

During these meetings, review the family's financial health, discuss any potential investment opportunities, and plan for any major financial decisions that need to be made. It's also the perfect opportunity to revisit your family's wealth preservation strategies and adjust them as necessary.

Moreover, use these meetings to celebrate achievements and milestones. Did someone make a smart investment? Did the family charity reach a new goal? Celebrate these wins together. It reinforces positive behaviours and keeps everyone motivated.

In closing, remember that passing on wealth is more than transferring assets. It's about passing on a legacy of knowledge, values, and structures that will support your heirs today, tomorrow, and many years into the future. By implementing thoughtful inheritance strategies, investing in financial education, and fostering open communication, you can ensure that your legacy is preserved and enhanced for generations to come.

Summary and Application Exercises

Congratulations on making it through this vital chapter on Legacy & Wealth Preservation. You've armed yourself with knowledge that not only prepares you for the future but ensures your legacy and wealth are protected and thoughtfully passed on. Let's boil down what we've covered into some practical steps you can take right away.

Planning for the Future:

1. **Estate Planning:** Schedule a consultation with an estate planner or solicitor. Even if you think it's early days, understanding your options will put you in control

2. **Creating a Will:** If you don't have a will, now's the time. If you do, review it. Circumstances change, and your will should reflect your current wishes and situation

3. **Trusts and Other Legal Tools**: Investigate if setting up a trust is right for your situation. Trusts can offer benefits like tax reductions and controlled distribution of your assets.

Protecting Your Assets:

1. **Insurance Options:** Review your current insurance policies. Are you covered comprehensively? Life, disability, and property insurance are key areas to consider

2. **Legal Protections for Wealth:** Consult with a solicitor to ensure your assets are shielded from potential lawsuits or claims. You might need to look into umbrella policies or restructuring asset ownership

3. **Safeguarding Digital Assets:** Secure and manage your digital presence. Ensure your digital assets like cryptocurrencies, online accounts, and intellectual properties are included in your estate plan.

Passing on Wealth:

1. **Strategies for Inheritance:** Define clear, legal pathways for your assets. Whether it's through direct gifts, trusts, or staggered distributions, make your intentions clear

2. **Educating the Next Generation on Wealth Management:** Consider setting up educational sessions with your heirs about financial management, investments, and the responsibilities of wealth

3. **Family Wealth Meetings:** Initiate regular family discussions about wealth. It's crucial everyone understands the value of your assets, the expectations, and how to sustain them.

Remember, wealth preservation isn't just about maintaining financial assets; it's about securing a future that aligns with your values and vision. Each step you take builds a bridge to a future where your legacy thrives. So, start these conversations, draft these documents, and make those decisions. Your future self, and your family, will thank you for it.

Notes & Reflections

Living the Millionaire Lifestyle

"Money is a terrible master but an excellent servant." - ***P.T. Barnum***

The Philosophy of Abundance

Welcome to a journey where the essence of richness extends beyond the confines of mere financial accumulation. Here, we delve into a mindset that reshapes what you pursue and cherish in life. Embracing this philosophy is the first step towards living not just a wealthy life, but a profoundly abundant one.

Embracing a Life of Plenty

Imagine waking up every day with the conviction that the world is brimming with opportunities and resources for everyone, including you. This is the heart of a life of plenty. It's about seeing abundance not as a finite pie, but as an ever-expanding universe of potential.

Breaking free from a scarcity mindset propels you beyond the fear of insufficiency. It's about understanding that by cultivating abundance within, you can generate it externally. Start by appreciating what you already have, from relationships to skills, and see them as foundational blocks to build more, rather than limitations confining you.

Cultivating an abundant mindset also involves gratitude. When you start your day with a sense of thankfulness for the smallest wins or possessions, you set a tone of contentment and openness, ready to receive and create more. It's about shifting focus from what you lack to what you possess and can offer to others.

Community plays a pivotal role here. Surround yourself with people who embody this abundance. Their perspectives and actions can inspire and challenge you to expand your own views about what is possible. Remember, abundance is contagious. By fostering relationships with those who also embrace this philosophy, you create a network of mutual support and inspiration.

The Balance Between Wealth and Happiness

You might wonder, how much wealth is enough? The balance between wealth and happiness is not about a specific number in your bank account, but about reaching a state where your financial status serves as a tool, rather than an end goal.

Financial freedom allows you to make choices that align with your passions and values. It enables you to say no to tasks or jobs that drain you and yes to those that enrich you. This freedom is a critical component of happiness. However, it's vital to recognise that the pursuit of wealth solely for accumulation often leads to a hollow victory. The real win is using your financial resources to support a life filled with joy and purpose.

Achieving this balance requires introspection. What makes you genuinely happy? Is it time with family, travel, or pursuing a hobby? Money can fund these passions, but without them, it merely accumulates. Define what happiness means to you and use your wealth as a means to cultivate these joys rather than substituting them with material gains.

It's also essential to set boundaries. Wealth can lead to overindulgence if not checked. The key is to enjoy the fruits of your labour without letting them consume you. Can you find pleasure in simple joys while also savouring the rewards of your hard work? This balance is not only achievable but necessary for a truly abundant life.

Redefining Success

In an abundant life, success is not measured by comparison but by personal fulfilment and growth. Redefining success on your terms involves understanding your values and aligning your goals with them. It's about writing your own story of success, one where you are the protagonist who defines victory.

This personal definition of success might look different from traditional views. Perhaps success to you means having the flexibility to work remotely, spend more time with loved ones, or engage in philanthropy. It's about creating a life that reflects your priorities and values, not society's.

Consider also the legacy you wish to leave. How do you want to be remembered? By redefining success, you focus on making an impact that resonates with your deepest values. Whether it's through mentorship, innovation, or kindness, your unique contribution to the world is a true measure of success.

Achievement in this sense is not a final destination but a continuous journey. It evolves as you grow and expand your horizons. Keep setting goals that challenge and fulfil you, and success becomes a path of continual satisfaction and surprise.

By adopting the philosophy of abundance, you transform not only your own life but also influence those around you. It's a philosophy that encourages not just personal wealth, but a richly lived life. Embrace this abundance with open arms and an open heart, and watch as the world opens its treasures in return.

Sustainable Wealth

Maintaining Wealth Over Time

Creating wealth is one thing, but maintaining it over the years requires a mix of discipline, foresight, and adaptability. You might think of it as cultivating a garden. It's not just about planting seeds; it's about nurturing the plants, watching out for pests, and continuously adapting to the weather patterns.

One key strategy is diversification. Don't put all your eggs in one basket, as the old saying goes. Spread your investments across different asset classes, such as stocks, bonds, real estate, and perhaps even some alternative investments like cryptocurrencies or commodities. The right mix should reflect your risk tolerance, financial goals, and the economic landscape. Diversification helps to buffer your wealth against the volatility of markets. When one investment performs poorly, another might thrive, balancing out the potential losses.

Another aspect of maintaining wealth is asset allocation. This isn't a set-it-and-forget-it strategy. Regular reviews and adjustments are crucial as your financial goals evolve over time and as you move through different stages of life. What works for you in your thirties might not suit your needs when you approach retirement.

Lastly, never underestimate the power of reinvestment. When your investments yield returns, reinvesting these gains can compound your wealth significantly over the years. It's like rolling a snowball down a hill; as it rolls, it picks up more snow, growing bigger and faster. Reinvestment can work much the same way with your wealth.

Avoiding Common Financial Pitfalls

Financial freedom is as much about avoiding mistakes as it is about making wise decisions. One of the most common traps is lifestyle inflation. As your wealth increases, it's tempting to increase your spending proportionally. This can be a slippery slope. Before you know it, your increased income is swallowed up by higher living expenses, which does nothing to increase your net worth.

To avoid this, keep a keen eye on your budget regardless of how much money you start making. It's fine to reward yourself and improve your standard of living, but do it judiciously. Remember, true financial independence isn't about flaunting wealth but securing it so that you can live comfortably and stress-free in the long term.

Debt management is another critical area. While not all debt is bad (think mortgages or business loans that potentially increase in value), consumer debt typically comes with high interest rates and can hinder your ability to build wealth. If you have debt, especially high-interest debt, make it a priority to pay it off as quickly as possible. Consider strategies like debt consolidation or refinancing to lower interest rates and reduce monthly payments.

Finally, don't fall for the trap of short-term thinking. The allure of quick returns can be tempting, but wealth is most commonly built and maintained through long-term, consistent strategies. Be wary of investment opportunities that promise high returns with little or no risk. If it sounds too good to be true, it probably is. Instead, focus on building a robust financial foundation that can withstand the ups and downs of economic cycles.

Staying Informed and Adaptable

The financial landscape is constantly changing. New technologies, shifting market trends, and global economic shifts can all affect your financial strategy. Staying informed is not about reacting to every piece of news but about understanding how these changes can impact your financial goals.

One effective way to stay informed is to allocate regular time each week to read up on financial news and trends. Follow reputable financial news sources, listen to podcasts, and perhaps subscribe to newsletters from trusted financial analysts. However, it's crucial to remain critical and discerning about the information you consume, focusing on how it applies to your personal financial situation.

Being adaptable is also crucial. This doesn't mean overhauling your financial strategy based on every market fluctuation, but rather being willing to make adjustments as significant changes in your life or the economy occur. This could mean rebalancing your investment portfolio, altering your retirement savings plan, or changing your budget to accommodate a new family member or career change.

Moreover, consider the impact of technology on personal finance. From apps that help you track your spending and investments in real time to platforms that automate savings and investments, leveraging technology can enhance your ability to maintain and build wealth.

In conclusion, sustainable wealth isn't just about accumulating assets but about managing them wisely through all seasons of life. By diversifying your investments, avoiding financial pitfalls, and staying informed and adaptable, you can protect and grow your wealth effectively. Remember, sustainable wealth is not just a means to an end but a way to ensure a secure, prosperous future where you can continue to live out your dreams without financial worry.

Enjoying Your Wealth

So, you've climbed the financial mountain and now you're perched at the summit, looking down at the sprawling landscape of wealth you've accumulated. It's quite the view, isn't it? But what's the point of reaching this peak if you can't enjoy the panorama? Wealth isn't just about accumulation; it's equally about utilisation, enjoyment, and responsible management. Let's explore how you can live richly, savour your success, and still maintain a balanced, mindful approach to your newfound affluence.

Responsible Luxury

Luxury, a term often synonymous with excess, need not be wasteful or ostentatious. Think of responsible luxury as the art of indulging wisely. It's about choosing quality over quantity and valuing experiences and goods that truly enhance your life and align with your values.

For instance, consider the car you drive. While a flashy sports car might scream 'wealth', a high-quality, well-engineered vehicle that balances performance with environmental impact could be a smarter choice. It says you value sophistication and responsibility.

Similarly, when it comes to your home, sustainable luxury can be your mantra. Investing in energy-efficient appliances, solar panels, or even a rainwater harvesting system doesn't just reduce your carbon footprint; it also trims your utility bills in the long term. Plus, there's a certain satisfaction in knowing that your luxury is not at odds with the planet's well-being.

When it comes to fashion, opt for brands that are transparent about their supply chains and committed to ethical practices. Not only will you look good, but you'll also feel good knowing your choices are contributing to fair labour practices and reduced waste.

Responsible luxury also extends to how you treat yourself. Regular health check-ups, spa retreats, or even organic meal kits are all ways to pamper yourself without guilt. After all, the greatest luxury you can afford is a long, healthy life.

Travel and Experiences

Now, let's talk about using your wealth to broaden your horizon—quite literally. Travel is one of the most enriching ways to spend your money, and not just in a figurative sense. It's about creating memories, gaining new perspectives, and experiencing life beyond your comfort zone.

Start by crafting travel experiences that are as unique as your financial journey. This doesn't mean you need to jet off to a new country every month. It's about quality and depth. Spend several weeks in a single location, immerse yourself in the local culture, learn the language, or volunteer. These experiences provide a richer return on investment than any luxury resort.

Consider eco-tourism or destinations that promote sustainability. Places like Costa Rica, known for its rainforest conservation efforts, or Bhutan, with its focus on gross national happiness, offer profound travel experiences that align with a lifestyle of responsible wealth.

And don't forget about the less tangible journeys. Workshops or retreats focused on personal development, be it mindfulness, cooking, or photography, can be transformative. They not only enrich your skill set but also provide valuable networking opportunities with like-minded individuals who share your values and interests.

Balancing Enjoyment with Prudence

Finally, enjoying your wealth also means managing it wisely. It's easy to get caught up in the euphoria of financial success and start splurging. However, true financial mastery is maintaining that delicate balance between enjoying your wealth and growing it.

Set up a budget for luxuries. It might seem counterintuitive to budget for indulgences, but it's a strategy that ensures you enjoy your wealth without compromising your financial health. Allocate a portion of your income to 'fun money'—this is your licence to splurge, guilt-free, whether it's on fine dining, gadgets, or art.

Invest in experiences and assets that appreciate or at least hold their value. Art, for instance, can be a great investment. Not only does it beautify your home, but it also has the potential to appreciate over time. Similarly, investing in real estate in emerging markets can offer both personal enjoyment and a sound return on investment.

Most importantly, ensure you have a robust financial plan in place. Continue to consult with financial advisors to keep your financial strategies responsive to changes in the market and in your personal life. Protect your assets through appropriate insurance and a well-thought-out estate plan. This ensures that you not only enjoy your wealth but also safeguard it for future generations.

In embracing these practices, you'll find that enjoying your wealth responsibly not only secures your financial future but also amplifies the joy and satisfaction derived from every pound spent. After all, wealth is not just about having great resources; it's about having the wisdom to use them well.

Summary & Application Exercises

Congratulations on navigating through the critical aspects of living the millionaire lifestyle. Embracing this journey isn't just about accumulating wealth; it's about crafting a life rich in experiences and sustained by wise choices. Let's distil what we've covered into practical steps you can take starting today.

Firstly, adopt the Philosophy of Abundance. Begin by recognising that abundance isn't merely financial; it's a mindset. Start each day by jotting down three things you are grateful for. This simple practice shifts your focus from scarcity to abundance, making you more open to opportunities. Also, redefine success on your own terms. What does a truly successful life look like to you beyond the financial figures? Sketch this vision out and refer back to it as you make decisions.

Moving on to Sustainable Wealth, the goal is not just to gain wealth but to maintain it. This requires continuous education. Commit to reading one financial book or listening to a relevant podcast each month. Knowledge is your greatest ally. Additionally, review your financial plans quarterly. This isn't just about checking your progress, but also about adapting to any changes in your personal circumstances or the economic landscape.

Finally, when it comes to Enjoying Your Wealth, remember that responsible luxury is key. Allow yourself the comforts and luxuries your financial position affords, but always with mindfulness and responsibility. Plan a trip that not only indulges your senses but also enriches your understanding of the world. Balance these experiences with prudence; always ensure that your spending aligns with your long-term financial goals.

Remember, the path to financial freedom isn't paved with occasional grand gestures, but with consistent, informed, and mindful actions. Take these steps seriously, and you're not just living the millionaire lifestyle; you're mastering it.

Notes & Reflections

Embracing Your Financial Freedom

As you turn the pages of this transformative journey, remember that each chapter was designed to equip you with the tools necessary to sculpt a future rich in financial freedom and abundant in opportunities. You've explored various dimensions of financial intelligence and personal growth, setting the stage for a life redefined by empowerment and economic independence.

The essence of this journey is not merely about accumulating wealth, but about mastering the intricate dance of sustaining and growing it. You have been equipped with the knowledge to shift your money mindset, develop habits that foster wealth, accelerate your income, and break free from the chains of debt. Now, the path forward beckons you to apply these insights and forge your financial destiny.

Financial freedom is more than a destination—it's a continuous pursuit that challenges you to apply learned principles consistently and innovatively. As you stand on the brink of this new beginning, consider how the foundations laid by your newfound knowledge can transform not just your bank account but your life.

The power of fearless finances is not just in overcoming the anxiety surrounding money but in embracing it as a tool for creating the life you've always envisioned. Imagine a future where financial worries do not constrain your choices—an existence where your financial resources serve not as a source of stress but as a springboard for achieving your dreams.

Moreover, wealth is not solely about personal gain; it's about creating a positive impact that transcends individual accomplishment. With financial stability comes the opportunity to contribute to your community, support causes you are passionate about, and help others find their path to financial enlightenment. This ripple effect of good, driven by your achievements, can be one of your most significant legacies.

However, the journey to financial mastery does not end here. It is an ongoing process of learning, adapting, and overcoming. The world of finance is ever-evolving, and staying informed and agile is key to continuing your growth. As markets fluctuate and new financial tools and technologies emerge, your ability to navigate these changes with confidence and foresight will be crucial.

Should you find yourself seeking guidance as you continue this journey, remember that help is just a click away. Whether you are looking to refine your strategies, explore new financial avenues, or simply seek reassurance on your path, professional help can provide you with the insight and support necessary to navigate complex financial landscapes confidently.

Remember, every investment in your financial literacy is an investment in your future. The principles and strategies you've absorbed are the keys to unlocking doors to opportunities you might never have imagined. Use them wisely, and continue to build on them. Your financial future is not set in stone—it is clay, ready to be moulded by your hands.

In closing, let this book serve not merely as a manual but as a manifesto—a declaration of your potential to achieve financial freedom and a prosperous, purpose-driven life. As you forge ahead, keep the lessons you've learned close to your heart. Let them guide your decisions, inspire your ambitions, and remind you of the power you hold to shape your destiny.

Your financial journey is uniquely yours, but you do not walk it alone. Millions are on this path, each with their dreams, challenges, and successes. Draw inspiration from them, as they will from you, and together, let's redefine what it means to live a life of financial freedom.

Go forth with courage, with purpose, and most importantly, with the knowledge that your financial future is bright, limitless, and entirely within your contro

Notes & Reflections

Notes & Reflections

Notes & Reflections

www.ingramcontent.com/pod-product-compliance
Lightning Source LLC
Chambersburg PA
CBHW071830210526
45479CB00001B/64